JULY 23, 2023
FOR EMILY—
WITH BLESSINGS FOR YOUR JOURNEY ----

AND SO I WALKED:

REFLECTIONS ON CHANCE, CHOICE, AND THE CAMINO DE SANTIAGO

AND SO I WALKED:

Reflections on Chance, Choice, and the Camino de Santiago

A memoir

by

ANNE GARDNER

Adelaide Books

New York / Lisbon

2022

AND SO I WALKED:
REFLECTIONS ON CHANCE, CHOICE,
AND THE CAMINO DE SANTIAGO
A memoir
By Anne Gardner

Copyright © by Anne Gardner
Cover design © 2022 Adelaide Books

Published by Adelaide Books, New York / Lisbon
adelaidebooks.org
Editor-in-Chief
Stevan V. Nikolic

For any information, please address Adelaide Books
at info@adelaidebooks.org
or write to:
Adelaide Books
244 Fifth Ave. Suite D27
New York, NY, 10001

ISBN: 978-1-956635-94-2

Printed in the United States of America

For my mother, who inspired and nurtured in me the three guideposts of my life – a love of reading, a sense of adventure, and a devout faith. And for my father, whose life of quiet dignity and courage I have tried my best to emulate. You have always been my lodestar, even now.

For my dear friend Carmel, who first told me of the Camino. My only regret is that we never had the chance to experience it together.

And finally, for the other members of the "Fab Five." I literally couldn't have done it without you.

With all my love,

¡Buen Camino!

Contents

Author's Note

The writing of this book was aided significantly by notes I kept while walking the Camino.

This account has also been supplemented with information contained in John Brierley's hiking classic, *A Pilgrim's Guide to the Camino de Santiago*. Brierley's text was the only reading material I carried while traversing the Camino, an investment well worth its weight. Through Brierley's meticulously researched book, I have been able to verify mileage totals, elevation heights and, on occasion, gleaned a few historical morsels that provided a more fulsome context for my contemporary experience.

In addition, post-pilgrimage conversations with my fellow hikers sparked memories of the trip, reminding me of details and stories I might otherwise have forgotten. I am grateful to each of my fellow travelers for adding this much-needed grist and flavor to the text.

Finally, the more personal portions of this book are reliant almost exclusively on my own recollection. While others may have experienced or remember these events differently, the chapters that follow recount how these stories live on in my own heart and mind. I ask the indulgence of my readers, particularly the members of my own family, to trust that, in the retelling of these narratives, I am telling my *own* truth, flawed though it may be.

Advent

n. Arrival. Past participle of *advenire*, to come to.
Any coming or arrival.

Sad News

"It was the best of times, it was the worst of times, it was the age of wisdom, it was the age of foolishness, it was the epoch of belief, it was the epoch of incredulity, it was the season of Light, it was the season of Darkness, it was the spring of hope, it was the winter of despair, we had everything before us, we had nothing before us, we were all going direct to heaven, we were all going direct the other way."

—Charles Dickens, *A Tale of Two Cities*

Armed with a fistful of quarters, I slid wearily into the plastic seat in front of me. For more than a week, we had walked the dirt-covered paths of northeastern Spain without the benefit of a newspaper, cell tower, or the internet. But now, a darkened computer screen was perched on the table across from my battered chair, an oasis amidst my technological desert. I dropped a few coins into the box affixed to the side of the terminal. A familiar blue haze began to flicker. My umbilical cord to the modern-day world had been revived.

A few keystrokes brought me to my email, now jammed with messages. I scrolled quickly, sifting through the assorted collection of ads, airline promotions, and automated reminders.

But then a line rose up from the sea of ink, catching my eye. I felt my brow furrow. The subject line read simply, "sad news." I clicked cautiously on the entry and scanned the first two lines. I never reached the rest, the remaining text now blurred by a trickle of tears.

> "I am so sorry to have to communicate this via email, but I have some terribly sad news to share. CeCe took her life this weekend."

A friend had written this missive from deep in the bowels of Harvard Medical School. For more than a decade he and I, along with CeCe and countless others, had been colleagues at another of Harvard's graduate programs. Our office bubbled with the kind of energy and unbridled exuberance reserved only for the young. We were like bright copper pennies back then, shimmering with possibility. Invincible, or so I thought.

Now, thousands of miles from Cambridge, I sat alone as the first quivers of dusk began to descend. I had come to Spain in hopes of traversing the famed pilgrimage route known as El Camino de Santiago de Compostela. I had allocated 40 days for the roughly 500-mile journey, grateful to join the tens of thousands of like-minded pilgrims who had come to this same expanse of sacred ground.

But as the light began to dim that night, I felt my lungs deflate, turning my breath into sharp, shallow gasps. My legs felt like lead beneath me. And then, just as quickly as my tears appeared, they evaporated. Disbelief now replacing my initial shock. Clear-eyed once again, I read those opening lines a second, and then a third, and then a fourth time. It was as if my brain had short-circuited. *I must have missed something*, I thought. *Surely there must be some sort of explanation.*

But my scrutiny revealed nothing further. No matter how many times I read the message, in the end, CeCe was still gone and I remained, panting through a hollow chest.

I'm not sure how much time passed, but eventually the others in my group came to find me. While they were soaking their tender feet in the cool water of the hostel's fountain, I had gone to check if access to the internet was available. When I didn't return, they grew worried.

Soon enough they discovered me, sitting rigid and glassy-eyed in front of the monitor. I turned to face them as they approached. I remember thinking I sounded remarkably calm as I told them of CeCe's death. My tone was robotic, strangely detached and devoid of emotion.

I saw the smiles slide from their faces as I relayed the news, concern now where joy had been. They stiffened, unsure of their next move in this delicate dance we had begun. Their gaze drifted downwards. An uneasy silence hovered over us.

If they were looking to me to provide direction, they were barking up the wrong tree.

Their leader had suddenly lost her way.

The Road Not Taken

"Two roads diverged in a wood, and I -
I took the one less traveled by,
And that has made all the difference."
—Robert Frost, *The Road Not Taken*

The day had started ordinarily enough.

Streaks of sunlight crept across my cot, rousing me from slumber. Soon enough, the rustle of harried packing filled the bunkroom. Many of my fellow pilgrims – *peregrinos*, as the Spaniards called us – were eager to be on their way. I quickly discovered this was a common practice, as if the Camino were a race rather than a pilgrimage. Disciples of this school of thought would bolt upright at the crack of dawn, ram their belongings into their rucksack, and set out at a feverish pace. They traveled light, both for speed and convenience. But their approach was imbued with an aggressiveness that made me wonder if they had come to do battle with the Camino. While impressed with their determination, I remained confused by their motivation. True, the Camino was a formidable foe. But in trying to dominate their would-be adversary, weren't they missing the point? In their rush to reach the end, they seemed, at least to me, to be foregoing the blessings of the journey.

Others stepped more gingerly, slowed by age or blisters or both. Many of these sojourners had packs, both literal and figurative, that were far too heavy for such an arduous endeavor. They were carrying too much, hoping for too much, expecting the Camino to be their salvation as well as their solace. Fatigue overtook this group almost immediately, their stooped shoulders and bloodied feet sure signs of hearts both too full and too empty.

Indeed, there seemed as many approaches to walking the Camino as there were pilgrims. My own group of five – Sascha, Jess, Meredith, Beth, and myself – was a good example of this kind of diversity. Confident and virile, Sascha had taken on the Camino with the kind of bravado typical of an adolescent. But after walking the first 60 miles (100 km) either barefoot or in flip flops, he had begun to experience the first painful pangs of shin splints. Hoping to give his tender legs a reprieve, he elected to ride the local bus that day, promising to meet us at an agreed-upon endpoint. A wise choice, I thought.

At first blush, his decision to traverse the next segment alone gave me pause. But I did my best to shake off my reticence with a double-barreled dose of optimism and naiveté. *He'll be fine*, I whispered to myself. His Spanish was decent enough. He was unusually mature for his age, despite this latest attempt to tap his inner Tom Sawyer. With Sascha headed to find the nearest bus stop, the rest of us began the long and slow ascent out of Navarette.

Jess and Meredith had fared much better by this point in the trip. Both remained unfazed by the daily mileage totals or the weight of their towering backpacks. They too were young and fit, but a bit more strategic than Sascha when it came to crunching miles. Careful to hydrate and pacing themselves accordingly, they were both fast as rabbits and tenacious as turtles.

My wife Beth and I, decades older than the others, took the "slow and steady" approach. We walked, we schmoozed, we took in the scenery. The day was plenty long enough, we assured ourselves. There was no need to rush. Although we were still in the nascent days of our adventure, everything was going according to plan.

A few hours later, our foursome reached the winsome hamlet of Ventosa, distinguishable only by its small and bustling café. We lumbered in, quickly jettisoning our packs to a side alcove just inside the front door. With the exception of Jess, each of us had nibbled on a spare granola bar as we walked, the morning sun warming our shoulder blades as we headed west. Jess' energy was based on adrenaline alone. Unfortunately, by the time we stopped for breakfast, she was not only hungry but also a bit nauseous. While she headed for the bathroom, the rest of us made a beeline for the counter. Within minutes, we were crouched around a small wooden table. Steam rose lazily from the coffee mugs gathered between us, reddening our cheeks. We greedily stabbed at a heaping pile of fried eggs, served with triangles of toast slathered in raspberry jam. After hours of exertion, however, I was in the mood for something a tad less greasy. Foregoing the traditional breakfast fare, I ordered a tuna sandwich. The others predictably wrinkled their noses at my choice, leaving me to eat in peace.

Jess eventually found her way to the table and absent-mindedly began to munch on a leftover piece of bread. With a robust combination of protein, carbohydrates, and caffeine now coursing through our veins, my crew seemed ready to tackle the rest of the day. Refreshed and satiated, I stood up, eager to resume our walk.

But Beth's appetite to continue had waned considerably over the course of our meal. During those first few days she, like Sascha, had developed an injury. A number of angry-looking blisters had bubbled up on the bottoms of her feet. This was the most common ailment to befall those out on the trail, and it was not one to be underestimated. Hot spots, left unattended, quickly developed into wounds that sidelined even the heartiest of hikers. Everyone had a homespun remedy for such situations, including Beth. But despite a steady application of moleskin and Vaseline, her blisters had only worsened. Every step she took was excruciating. She decided that morning's climb was all she could muster. As we prepared to leave the café, she announced she too would find a bus to take her to Azofra.

Out of nowhere, I felt a surge of disapproval rise like bile in my throat. Beth had no knowledge of Spanish and would be further hampered by her poor sense of direction. Fending for herself seemed like a terrible idea to me. I had insisted right from the start that we travel *together*, both for our protection and my own peace of mind. Walking the Camino had been my idea after all. Although each of us had agreed to join of our own accord, I still felt responsible for the group. Even more so for Beth.

My "togetherness strategy" was unraveling at record speed. In retrospect, this shouldn't have come as much of a surprise. Given the wide gap in our ages, a span that ranged from 18 to 58, keeping a uniform pace was nearly impossible. Compounding the problem was a corresponding lack of fitness. Crow's feet make for slow feet. A fact I could no longer deny.

Sascha and Meredith, the two teenagers, had fallen into an easy rhythm from the beginning. On most days, they walked together. Beth, Jess, and I moved in and out of pairings, depending on our energy level and the elevation of that day's route. As a result, by the end of the first mile or so, our group had often drifted apart. Hoping to maintain some semblance of cohesion, I knew we needed a plan to accommodate our various gaits and abilities. I had been warned by more experienced hikers of the temptation to alter one's pace once on the trail. Concerns about securing one of the limited beds at the next hostel might cause you to walk faster than you normally would. Conversely, wanting to continue a conversation with a fellow pilgrim might convince you to drop into a lower gear. But the slightest adjustment to your stride could very well strain your legs, hips, and knees in ways that would result in injury. Finding a solution to this conundrum became my top priority.

In the end, we settled on a tiered approach. Each morning we selected a handful of pre-determined points where we agreed to stop. These landmarks served as resting spots and as a mechanism by which we could track the progress of the group. Once the last straggler had arrived at the appointed marker, the others were free to set off once more. With no maps, no cell phone reception, and a distinctly remote landscape ahead of us, this rudimentary method of herding seemed the best option.

While I cherished the silence and autonomy of strolling at my own pace, I still looked forward to these touchstone moments sprinkled throughout the day. Some of my favorite memories of the pilgrimage are of telling stories under the shade of a tree, sharing a slice of apple or cheese with my pilgrim family during our mini reunions. Everyone agreed this new strategy provided just the right amount of freedom and accountability. Instead of being frustrated or annoyed, Sascha, Meredith, and Jess embraced the more languid pacing. Knowing they could easily catch up, I often passed them while each took time for other endeavors. I would come around a corner to discover Sascha sitting on a stone wall, writing in his journal. Jess would drift off the trail to take photographs of churches or fields of flowers. Meredith, eager to meet other hikers, used the time to strike up conversation at the local potable water fountain. The plan was working. My nerves were steadied. The group's movement ebbed and flowed organically and safely.

But now our arrangement was in jeopardy. Beth was an adult, a grown woman who had single-handedly raised two children. She was certainly capable of assessing her own injuries and deciding on a prudent course of action. Both her feet were red and raw. Continuing to walk would only worsen their condition. She had reached her breaking point.

Deep inside, I heard a warning bell begin to ring. How would she possibility navigate this next stretch without knowing in which direction to head nor having the ability to ask? The plan to strike out on her own seemed imprudent at best and dangerous at worst. There was something else at play, something I was ashamed to admit. During the previous two days, I had ridden the bus with Beth for short jaunts, as the first of her blisters began to appear. Despite my empathetic aura, in actuality I was growing increasingly resentful. Part of my interest in walking the Camino was to experience its grueling physical demands. With every mile that passed under those wheels, I felt like I was cheating; cheating myself out of what I had come to Spain to accomplish.

While I stewed on this dilemma, an unexpected solution suddenly appeared. "I'll go with Beth," Meredith chirped. "I want to take a break anyway, so I'll ride the bus with her."

I glanced over with a look of stunned disbelief. Meredith, *at 18*, needed a break? Was my petulant visage *that* obvious? Was she stepping in so I wouldn't have to? Or was the idea of an afternoon spent napping and reading too enticing for Meredith to resist? I didn't know the answer and, frankly, I didn't care.

Meredith was an old soul, confident and comfortable in foreign environments. She had a good command of both French and Spanish. I was convinced Beth would be safe with her.

Now free of both responsibility and guilt, I could barely contain my excitement. The day's remaining nine miles stretched out like a yellow brick road in front of me. The Camino was calling, and I intended to answer.

The Dream

"To everything there is a season, and a time to every purpose under the heaven."

—*Ecclesiastes 3:1 (KJV)*

Despite having been raised in the Catholic church and educated by Jesuits, I had never heard of the Camino until I was well into my 40s. My childhood, like many in my Irish-Catholic neighborhood, was filled with the standard lexicon of religious devotion – rosary beads, plaid skirts, the *Baltimore Catechism*, and an unwavering allegiance to President John F. Kennedy. I had also been schooled on some of the more significant historical moments of my faith tradition, including the appearance of the Virgin Mary at Lourdes, the frightful carnage of the Crusades, and the less-than-savory lives of a number of the popes. And yet somehow the rambling path to Santiago had never appeared on any syllabus of mine, inside the classroom or out.

Oddly enough, I first learned of the Camino while attending a cocktail party. I was hunkered down in the corner of my new boss's living room. On the job for only a few weeks,

I was desperately trying to balance a small plate of cheese and crackers on my knees without embarrassing myself. My colleagues buzzed around me, as if unaware of my plight. With drinks in hand and heads tilted in animated conversation, they paid me no heed.

Out of the corner of my eye, I noticed one of the guests heading in my direction. She was from Cuba and, after discovering I was a minister, excitedly told me of her desire to walk El Camino de Santiago de Compostela. When I returned her enthusiasm with a blank stare, she launched into a detailed description of the famous pilgrimage.

The more she spoke, the more enamored I became. Having a body type better suited to endurance than speed, I had always been drawn to long-distance challenges. In my mid-30s, I participated in a number of Avon Breast Cancer events, walking 60 miles over the course of just three days. It was a good match for me at the time, offering a serious physical challenge while raising funds for a cause in which I believed. But *this* walk – some 500 miles across an unfamiliar landscape with virtually no support systems – presented an entirely different kind of trial. Particularly now that I was on the cusp of turning 50.

Leaning forward, I lowered my glass onto a nearby tabletop. I fired a barrage of questions, eager to keep the banter flowing. But instead of being deterred by the frightful details, I felt my heart begin to stir. Who *was* this woman? And why was I so drawn to this crazy notion of walking across Spain? Hoping not to appear too much like a Pollyanna, I told her the Camino sounded like something I might like to try. Her eyes sparkled. "I thought so," she murmured. Without knowing it, my newest quest had begun.

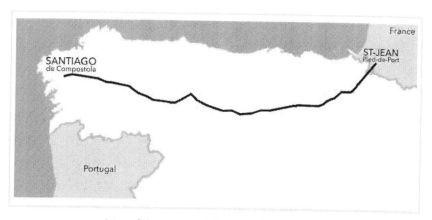

Map of the Camino de Santiago de Compostela

I forsook the circulating platters of crudités to focus instead on this fascinating story of the Camino. Santiago, as I soon learned, is the terminus of this famed pilgrimage, revered as the final resting place of St. James the Apostle. Prior to being beheaded in Jerusalem by Herod Agrippa I, James traveled to the Iberian Peninsula to preach the "good news" to members of the then-fledgling Christian church. As lore would have it, his remains were transported back to Spain following his martyrdom. Upon reaching Santiago, the remnants were then buried alongside two of his compatriots and left undisturbed until the ninth century.

It is said the hermit Pelagius finally discovered the tomb, led to its location by a field of stars he saw in a dream. This encounter was authenticated by King Alphonso II who subsequently declared James to be the patron saint of Spain. A monastery was built on the site in his honor. Soon thereafter, a small village, aptly named Campus de la Stella (Field of Stars), came into being. For Christians, Santiago was now holy ground.

During the Middle Ages, the town became a popular pilgrimage destination as the faithful made their way across Spain to honor the apostle, to deepen their own spiritual lives and, in some cases, to receive indulgences (an ecclesiastical pardon granted in exchange for a good deed or fee) from the Catholic Church. But the number of pilgrims dropped precipitously over time. By the mid-1980s, those receiving their *Compostela* (proof of their completed journey) fell to just under 2,500 per year. It was also a decidedly non-American endeavor, with U.S. citizens comprising a negligible 1 to 2 percent of all participants.

It's little wonder that the reaction I received from colleagues and friends alike upon declaring my intent to walk the Camino fell somewhere between ignorance and disbelief. "Why would you want to do *that?*" many opined.

Good question, I thought. Good question ...

Utah Beach

"O God, that men should put an enemy in their mouths to steal away their brains!"

—William Shakespeare, *Othello*

Every adventure begins somewhere. Such is the case with this journey, the seeds of which initially took hold in the blood-soaked soil of Normandy.

I am my father's daughter. Unequivocally. Unabashedly. And without apology.

The older I get, the more similarities I see. It is from his root that this branch has taken shape.

My father was a quiet man. Nearly silent, actually. He grew up the only son and namesake of an abusive and drunken father. His mother, dutiful but withered, spent most of her marriage scared out of her wits. Born in 1917, my father came of age on the cusp of the Great Depression. Money was tight. Opportunities infrequent.

But that didn't stop those precious few dollars from being squandered. Just as quickly as my grandmother would earn a handful of coins sewing hems or re-attaching buttons, the money would disappear into the coffers of the nearest bar.

Whiskey. Always whiskey. Poured into a bottomless hole down my grandfather's gullet.

The constant sheen of liquor that clung to his skin only bolstered his swagger. Handsome and charming, he was all talk, my grandfather. But when his young family needed someone on whom to rely, when they needed some assurance of stability and safety during those very uncertain years, he turned out to be a paper tiger. With enough machismo to slap his cowering wife or rain haymakers down upon his young son, he was somehow never strong enough to earn a steady paycheck or keep a roof over the heads of his children.

My father, from a very early age, vowed he would never, *ever*, be like his father. It was a promise he would keep.

With rumblings of war rolling across the nations of Europe, my father enlisted in the army. Still in his teens, he was happy to put on the uniform. With the country awash in patriotic zeal, this was a real chance for him to alter the direction of his life. He would fight. But this time, he would play offense and not defense.

He was initially assigned to Camp Edwards in eastern Massachusetts, the first stop of a multi-year basic training cycle. Though his olive fatigues hung precipitously off his slender frame, he made a name for himself during his time there. His commanding officers saw how calm he remained under duress. He proved to be a talented marksman. Most importantly, he was reliable. He told the truth. And he inspired an instant rapport and trust with the men placed under his charge.

In the late spring of 1944, he and countless others found themselves wedged into the hulls of U.S. battleships headed to the shores of France. Part of the 83rd infantry division, he was among the swarm of soldiers who scrambled onto the beaches of Normandy. The few who survived made their way up and over the cliff's edge, headed toward the front lines.

Now on higher ground, my father led his platoon first to Sainte Mère Église, then to Carentan, and finally to the small town of Périers, just over 20 miles south of their landing spot on Utah Beach. Progress was exceedingly slow. It took days to gain each precious scrap of ground, crawling hour after hour through slit trenches dug alongside the hedgerows that delineated the fields of rural northwest France.

Unbeknownst to him, it would be a shorter stay than he anticipated. While hunkered down in a shallow trench, he was struck by the shards of an overhead mortar burst. The blast tore the flesh of his right leg and snapped his femur, leaving only a few tendons connecting his thigh to his lower leg. The shrapnel also created a gaping wound in his left calf. Crippled with pain, he lay motionless in the dirt.

As the blood poured from his wounds, a fellow soldier ran across the open field and dove into my father's foxhole. He quickly twisted his shirt into a makeshift tourniquet, temporarily stemming the flow. Dust clogged the air as the German onslaught continued. In the chaos, choices were limited. In the end, the decision was made to drag my father, now in shock, back towards the reinforced line of troops. A short while later, a medic at the 34th Evacuation Field Hospital performed a procedure known as a guillotine amputation, severing my father's right leg at mid-thigh.

He would remain unconscious for three days, and was eventually moved to a medical facility in England to continue his recovery. But the gash created by the amputation was so jagged it would take four months before the doctors could reattach the remaining flap of skin over the shattered bone. Bedridden and far from home, my father's days and nights stretched into one long blur. His career as an infantryman was over. The only question that remained was, what next?

At the tender age of 26, he had lost both his command and his leg. It was a moment that would change his life. And it was a moment that would change mine.

Careful What You Wish For

"Whenever I travel, I prefer to do it light."

—Shirley MacLaine, *The Camino: A Journey of the Spirit*

Perhaps the most famous account of walking the Camino was written by Shirley MacLaine, now equally as well-known as an Oscar-winning actress as she is for her avowed belief in reincarnation. MacLaine walked the Camino in 1994, and much of her book revolves around her spiritual experience of the pilgrimage – that is to say, around her experience of past lives. Despite this quirky lens, her musings on cyclical rebirth are not what I remember most from her manuscript. No, things much more mundane captured my attention. Things that kept the idea of hiking the Camino firmly rooted in the here and now.

Her cautionary soliloquy told of a trio of concerns: the ubiquitous presence of untethered, snarling dogs; her frequent inability to locate the trail's scalloped markers; and her near-constant angst over the weight of her backpack.

Like most pilgrims, MacLaine was obsessed with the size and girth of her pack. Most guidebooks advise would-be hikers not to carry more than 10 percent of their body weight in supplies and equipment. Quickly doing the math, MacLaine concluded this calculation would result in far too prodigious a burden to sustain over the long haul. She was determined to reduce the weight of her pack to under 10 pounds, which was an admirable but seemingly improbable goal from my perspective. No matter how often I sorted and thinned my "essentials," I never reached this anorexic level. I resolved to be content with a 15-pound goal, confident my sturdy frame could withstand that level of ballast. Even so, I found lugging around that much extra weight all day to be exhausting.

Back in Ventosa, the four of us, already minus a bus-bound Sascha, were still milling about outside the café. With MacLaine's exhortations fresh in my memory, I recognized an opportunity, perhaps my *only* opportunity, to rid myself of my pack. If Beth and Meredith stuck to the plan of riding to the day's final destination, perhaps they could take *all of our packs*, leaving Jess and me to walk the final 9.5 miles (15.2 km) with the meagerest of provisions.

Both readily agreed to act as our Sherpas. After grabbing a small water bottle and some food from our stash, I headed down the path with Jess, leaving Beth and Meredith to wait for their bus.

Our walk that afternoon was filled with beautiful vistas, winding grooves of dirt, and plenty of solitude. Only the sound of my labored breathing pierced the silence. We made two significant climbs that day; scaling the gradual incline of Alto Poyo de Roldan, followed by a thigh-burning ascent of the hill located on the far side of Nájera, the town just before Azofra. Given the gradient, it was a treat to be free of my belongings as I made my way up and over the sloped ground. At times it felt as if I were almost floating across the landscape, light in both spirit and body.

It was also one of the very few times I had a chance to walk only with Jess. As we journeyed, I found comfort in both the absence and presence of conversation. I remember thinking it was a great gift to have this time with my friend, unencumbered by the usual responsibilities that work and family bring. Instead of sharing gossip over a quick dinner, our palaver was allowed to marinate, evolving organically during the long stretches of silence.

This sort of dilatory meditation had become a familiar practice by the time I reached adulthood. When I was a young girl, my mother would often take me to a spit of hard-packed sand called Nantasket, a nearby beach that curled into the Atlantic Ocean just south of Boston. I was the daughter of two redheads, so my trips to the beach were reserved for autumn, well after the hordes of tanning teenagers had disappeared. Donning a windbreaker and baseball cap, rather than the customary layer of baby oil, I found my time at the water's edge to be imbued with tranquility. Every once in a blue moon, the sun would warm the water enough to lure me into the waves. But that was a rare occurrence at such a northern latitude. Despite my fascination with the swells and tide, the water was not my muse.

I came to the beach *to walk*.

Now surrounded by the arid hills of Spain's La Rioja province, the gentle whoosh of surf against sand had been replaced with a panoply of red poppies. The flowers dotted the fields in the thousands, blossoms clinging like drops of paint to the tips of the tall green stalks. On occasion, a soft puff of wind would bend a section this way or that. This mesmerizing patchwork extended all the way to the horizon, a view interrupted only by the wide earthen road of the Camino.

During the early portion of the day, Jess and I traversed the undulating hills flanked on all sides by these vivid splashes of red and green. But by the afternoon, the fields had been replaced by steep bluffs. Making matters worse, the vertical sections were covered with a layer of small, loose rock. Each step dislodged a small cascade of stones. Our progress slowed to a crawl as we simultaneously advanced and regressed on the slippery surface. Those last few miles proved quite a challenge.

By the time we arrived in Azofra, it was late. As was our practice, we made our way to the local church, the only structure present in every village, regardless of size. The Camino originated during the medieval era, which meant no matter how small or remote a town, it still had a church. To this day, most of the Camino is remarkably rural, comprised of a collection of communities the modern world has all but forgotten. Had it not been for the steady stream of pilgrims each year, many of these enclaves would have already disappeared. Reduced to dusty stopovers, they are home to a few shops, some gaunt livestock, the occasional stray dog, and a meager population of the very elderly. Despite this decline, churches remain at the heart of these towns. Like crumbs left by Hansel and Gretel, they continue to mark the way to Santiago.

Jess and I headed to the only church in sight, predictably located in the center of the village. Much to our surprise, no one was waiting for us. Although they had left hours earlier, Sascha, Meredith, and Beth were nowhere to be seen. While Jess poked her head inside the narthex, I circled around back. When we both reappeared at the chapel's front steps, neither of us had found them. Perhaps they had gone to reserve beds at the nearby hostel, we surmised. Let's wait awhile. Surely, they will be back soon.

Weary from the heat and our efforts, Jess and I lay down on the cool stone patio, in a shady patch at the top of the stairs. Time clicked by. Still, no one appeared. Even in our semi-drowsy state, there was no refuting our mounting worry. After an hour or so, we crossed the plaza to find something to eat. But not before taking a stone and scratching a message on the bottom step of the staircase.

"Jess and Anne were here. Gone to the bar to eat."

We had just enough money for two small salads and a drink. After placing our order, we passed the time by watching the small television set located high above the beer tap. The channel was tuned to the World Cup, and despite the fact it was the middle of the afternoon, every stool in the place was taken. Plenty more onlookers stood against the back wall, all held in rapt attention by the action, smoking nervously and clutching their mugs of ale. Whatever their usual responsibilities may have been, nothing was more important than watching their beloved team. Work would just have to wait.

Once our food arrived, I spent most of the time pushing the lettuce around my plate. I was too tired to eat and remained preoccupied with what might have happened to the others. Every so often one of us would broach the topic, but it didn't last for long. I realized my worry had turned into fear.

We left our remaining coins as a tip and returned to the church. Along the way, we checked the town's fountain before proceeding to the front of the building where we had scrawled our note. As we turned the final corner, I saw them – Meredith, Beth, and our four backpacks – all leaning up against the foundation of the building.

But instead of being relieved, a flash of annoyance came over me. I was unaccustomed to feeling helpless. For hours I had wrung my hands. More than once that day, I chastised myself for letting any of them out of my sight. If something went wrong, a good share of the fault would be mine. I convinced myself I was capable of controlling all the variables; ridiculous now in hindsight. But in the moment, it was all I could do to contain my temper.

So instead of flinging my arms around both of them and gushing about how grateful I was to see their shiny faces, I announced with a self-satisfied smirk how difficult a hike it had been. Beth looked at me and said simply, "I know." Haughtily I replied, "No, not the heat, the *walking*." To which she responded, "Yes, I know. We *walked*."

I snapped my head back in her direction, confusion now replacing my contempt.

And oh, what a walk it had been...

Strike Three

"It is our choices, Harry, that show what we truly are,
far more than our abilities."

—J.K. Rowling, *Harry Potter and the Chamber of Secrets*

Stripped of our cumbersome backpacks, Jess and I had easily scampered up the narrow path that led to Azofra. Beth and Meredith went in the opposite direction, back down the hill with our four packs in tow, headed for the only bus stop in Ventosa. The small bench adjacent to the bus route marker was empty. Undeterred, they sat down to wait. Every so often a car would pass, kicking up dirt into a swirling smoky cloud. But still, no bus.

In the distance, a large vehicle finally appeared on the horizon. Much relieved, Meredith stood and wandered out into the road. She raised her arm like a flag, and the bus dutifully stopped. After a bit of back and forth in Spanish, the driver was able to convey that Azofra was *not* on the day's route. Meredith returned to the bench to break the news to Beth. "Not to worry," she said serenely. "We'll just wait for the next one."

What they didn't know was that they had just seen the last bus that would travel down the road that afternoon. Azofra, like so many other towns on the Camino, was simply too far off the beaten path to warrant regular bus service. Unwittingly, they had swung and missed. Strike one.

Eventually, they trudged back up the hill to the café and asked the proprietor to call for a taxi. Soon enough the promised car came screaming up the street, abruptly lurching to a stop. But one look at the young and reckless driver convinced Beth that getting into the cab was not a good idea. When Meredith explained this to the driver, he erupted, demanding they pay a fee of 20 Euros simply because he had appeared. Beth balked, which made him even more irate, launching a torrent of words and gestures they could neither understand nor follow. Sensing an opportunity to force their hand, the driver grabbed Jess' pack off the top of the pile and flung it into the trunk, slamming the lid down with a loud bang.

No one knew what to do next. The driver refused to leave. Beth refused to pay. And the others in the restaurant began to avert their gaze from the looming international incident that was now unfolding. As if out of central casting, help arrived for the second time that day. A smartly dressed gentleman, replete with a fancy bow tie, inserted himself into the fray. He approached Beth and, in flawless English, offered some cultural expertise and a cooler head. After a short tête-à-tête, he confirmed what she had feared. It was indeed customary to compensate a driver, even if the anticipated ride was not taken. Beth grudgingly handed over the cash and Jess' belongings were released from the trunk. The driver raced off in a huff and Beth and Meredith were back to square one. Strike two.

Once again, they dragged the four packs back to the bus stop. An elderly couple, out for their daily stroll, had plopped down on the bench for a short reprieve. While there, Meredith struck up a conversation with the pair and learned no other buses were scheduled that day. Another dead end. Beth decided there was only one thing left to do. With no bus and no taxi service on which to rely, she proposed they hitchhike. Meredith was circumspect about this strategy, but Beth assured her that her thumb had bummed many a ride during the 1960s.

Surely it would not fail them now.

Despite her brimming confidence, this game plan failed as well. Squinting down the road, they saw nothing. No cars. No motorcycles. Not even a tractor. It had been nearly two hours since Jess and I had left the café and the heat of the day was upon them. They were officially stranded and plumb out of ideas.

Except, of course, for the most obvious one.

I Feel It in my Heart

"If you want to walk fast, walk alone.
If you want to walk far, walk together."

—*African Proverb*

It would be Meredith who would see them through. Slowly she rose from the bench and headed across the street toward Beth. "We have to walk," she said. "I feel it in my heart."

Walk *where*, Beth wondered. Surely she wasn't suggesting they walk all the way to Azofra? Still, there was something reassuring about the way Meredith spoke, a tone so grounded and steady that it drew her in. It was a preposterous idea really, and yet Beth found herself nodding.

They would walk. Somehow, they would walk.

The most pressing problem would be what to do with the two extra packs. Nearly 10 miles lay between Ventosa and Azofra. Between the blisters and the soaring temperatures, the remaining stretch would be difficult to traverse. But what were they *possibly* going to do with the packs? Just as they had run out of ideas for transportation, they also ran out of possible solutions to this latest quandary. Best not to overthink this one, they decided.

They would simply shoulder the additional weight. And they would try *very* hard not to think any more about it.

The first order of business was to drain the two water pouches tucked inside the spine of each backpack. This reduced the weight of each by nearly eight pounds. Beth and I had purchased the exact same equipment while back in the States, a mid-sized rucksack with padded shoulder straps and belt. This symmetry made the puzzle a bit easier to solve. First Beth secured her own pack. Then Meredith hoisted mine up to Beth's chest, looping her arms through the second pair of straps and snapping the waist belt of my pack just above her tailbone. Both packs were now positioned as mirrored duplicates, one on the front and one on the back. Beth was ready to give it a try.

Unfortunately, Jess' pack turned out to be far too large and unwieldly for this same trick. It seemed the only viable option was to lash the extra pack to the back of Meredith's. The bags protruded like two camel humps, a combined weight that bent Meredith into the shape of a question mark. Initially staggering by the heft, she found her sea legs after 10 or so yards. They were committed to their plan and resolved to see it through. Not that there was another alternative. The only way to leave Ventosa was by foot. They headed up the first hill, loaded to the gills.

It quickly became apparent that to survive this ordeal they would need a distraction, something potent enough to take their minds off the task at hand. So they did what countless other women have done when faced with such challenges. They talked. Every step of the way, they talked. Meredith told the story of how her parents met, a sweet and unexpected love story between her Pakistani Muslim father and her American-born Christian mother. She told of their uneasy compromise to raise Meredith within the tenets of Islam, a decision that almost stopped her from being allowed to come to Spain, so fearful was her father she might be converted while on such a traditionally Christian expedition.

The conversation moved next to the topic that monopolized the thoughts of nearly every teenager I knew: the relentless pressure to successfully navigate the college admissions process. For Meredith, like so many high-flying students, this meant acquiring a golden ticket to the most prestigious of institutions. For her family, that crowned jewel was Harvard, a quest that caused her so much anxiety she never spoke the name aloud, referring to the Cambridge institution only as "H." Despite the fact that plenty of other topflight programs – Emory, Michigan, Wellesley, and Duke – had flooded her inbox with letters of admission, her father's thirst for "H" remained.

She was the perfect child it seemed – well, almost – a deferential daughter who had spent her entire life trying to rise to her parents' expectations. But this time she had come up short. Without an offer from Harvard, the whole process had ground to a disappointing halt.

There was little margin for error in her life, a reality Meredith had understood long ago. But somehow, under the broad and azure skies of the Camino, her weariness began to subside. Even while struggling under the weight of her two enormous packs, Meredith felt strangely free. Perhaps this was part of what she had come to learn. That she was capable and she was enough. Just the way she was.

Beth already knew why she had come to the Camino. At 58, with two daughters and five grandchildren in her extended brood, she was happy and comfortable, but perhaps a bit complacent as well. Walking the Camino was not something she would have considered on her own. The heat, the rudimentary living conditions, even the walking itself held no allure for her. She knew she didn't *want* to do the walk, but that didn't keep her from wondering whether she still *could*.

Had she already turned that corner in her life, the one where caution overrules adventure? Did she secretly prefer the routine that kept her life predictable, even if her world was growing smaller because of it? When we first met, Beth told me a story about how she used to pray for patience. When her girls were young, this was a particularly frequent plea. Being a single parent and their sole provider had not been easy. Surely a few petitions sent heavenward couldn't hurt. But one day, she told a friend about this strategy and was summarily disavowed of it. "Asking for patience will only bring more trials," she warned. "How else would you know if your prayers were answered? Don't ask for something unless you're prepared to get it."

For Beth, making the decision to walk the Camino was a premeditated and carefully constructed prayer for strength. If she wanted to be stronger, to test her will and endurance, she would have to invite into her life a challenge of some significance. And so it was that her wish came true, just as she had prayed, that day in Ventosa.

They filled the afternoon with stories and laughter and soon enough found themselves in the town of Nájera. From there they were able to get a ride to Azofra, avoiding the last 3.5 miles (5.8 km) of the day's scheduled journey. But their relief quickly dissipated. They grew worried when they arrived at the church and found no one waiting. After checking each of the doors, Meredith came across our chalked note on the stairs. Reassured but exhausted, they decided against venturing into town to find whatever bar we were inhabiting. They would wait, and wait they did, until we finally returned to roost.

During my time on the Camino, as a spiritual discipline of sorts, I would ruminate on how my experience of the pilgrimage connected with the scriptural texts of my faith. Hearing the details of Beth and Meredith's hike that day, a tale of determination, creative problem solving, and faith, reminded me of the account of the paralytic man. It was a story I had heard countless times as a young girl while sitting with my mother in church. As a child, such dramatic tales captured my imagination. This was one of those days.

This biblical account (*New Revised Standard Version*, Mark 2:1–12 and Luke 5:17–26) tells of a man hoping to be noticed by Jesus, a charismatic leader reputed to have the power to heal the sick of their afflictions. The man had traveled from Capernaum to meet this mysterious medicine man. But the crowd surrounding Jesus had grown too large. Try as he might, the paralyzed man just couldn't imagine how to get close enough to even be noticed by Jesus, never mind healed. As he was constrained to a makeshift cot, his hopes appeared dashed.

But then a handful of others, sensing his desperation, concocted an unlikely plan. Together they lifted his stretcher and sliced their way through the assembled crowd. Still barred from entering the hut where Jesus resided, they hoisted the man above their heads and lowered him through a hole they had dug in the roof. Impressed by his resolve, Jesus rewarded the penitent man by granting him forgiveness. It's a fantastical narrative, a story of both faith and grit. And it's a reminder of how very much we are capable of, even when the obstacles ahead seem insurmountable.

True, the journey Beth and Meredith had taken that day was fueled by a different kind of desperation. And yet they too accomplished a feat so improbable it still boggles my mind.

Despite the fact our trip was less than a week old, I knew without a shadow of a doubt that Beth had just experienced the seminal moment of her Camino experience.

June 21st – the summer solstice, the longest day of the year, and the day I would learn my friend CeCe would see no other days – would be the moment of Beth's triumph. In taking on *my* burdens, she had realized she was strong enough to carry her own.

The magic of the Camino had begun.

Life or Limb

"There are things that everyone carries. I don't really know the
things inside my mother, but I know she feels so much more
than she says."

—George Hodgman, *Bettyville*

My father returned home from the war with a bronze star and a
purple heart. In short order, he had risen through the ranks and
been made an officer. Promoted to Major, his leadership and
bravery had been codified for all to see.

Despite incurring a permanent disability, he was allowed
to remain in the military. Back in the States, he accepted a desk
job at the Army's northeast headquarters in downtown Boston.
By this time, the military was what he knew, what he did, and
who he was. If it meant he would shuffle papers for the duration
of his career, that's what he would do.

He rented a small room in a nearby boarding house in order
to be close to work. Each flat had all the necessities – a bed, a
desk, a chair, and a closet. On many a night, his landlady made
a communal meal for her hodgepodge flock. It was a simple life,
uncomplicated by family responsibilities.

During this same period of time, my mother, 10 years my father's junior, had just enrolled at Emmanuel College, a women's school known largely for its humanities curriculum and Roman Catholic identity. Emmanuel was the first school of its kind in New England, founded in 1919 by the Sisters of Notre Dame de Namur. By the mid-1940s, Emmanuel still clung to its original mission. Servicing a largely working-class population, it was the preferred destination for many an immigrant's daughter. While progeny of Boston's elite headed to the Seven Sisters, Emmanuel kept its chin high and its standards higher.

Although they lived just a few miles from one another, my parents wouldn't meet until the early 1950s. My father lived a life of order and obedience, ruled by the code of the military. My mother, conversely, was hell-bent on coloring outside the lines. Refusing to acquiesce to a curriculum designed to train teachers, nurses, or nuns, my mother pushed to be recognized as a chemistry major. She was smart, blazingly so, with a fiery temperament to match. The youngest of six and the daughter of an Irish maid, she felt she had something to prove.

In the spring of 1949, she did just that. With degree in hand, she took a job working for Dr. Elliott Joslin, the same physician who would later open the first diabetes care facility in the world, a flagship clinic that now bears his name. But that wouldn't happen until 1956, the same year my mother and father married. Once a newlywed, she gave up her lab coat for a modest 1,280-square-foot ranch in the suburbs. But pursuing an Ozzie and Harriett lifestyle proved much more difficult than she had imagined. Her frustration, and subsequent anger, with a life dictated by the monotony of lawn care and laundry would build throughout the rest of her life. Although just an ember in those early years, her fury would later grow into a full-fledged fire.

The war took away my father's leg, but not his will. But marriage broke my mother's heart, no matter how much she insisted otherwise.

Ready, Set, GO

"Own only what you can carry with you: know language,
know countries, know people.
Let your memory be your travel bag."

—Aleksandr Solzhenitsyn

The plan to actually walk the Camino, a notion that began as just a bit of cocktail-party banter, took two full years to come to fruition. In the meantime, the idea quietly marinated and bubbled on the back burner of my imagination. Every now and then I would realize I was thinking about the possibility, dare I say it the *probability*, of undertaking such an epic adventure. I rolled the idea around in my head, considering it from every angle. Would I physically be up to the task? What sort of training would I need to be adequately prepared? What if I were to be injured? How would I muster the mental and emotional grit such an endeavor required? Would my marriage be able to withstand the strain of my extended absence? Even more complicating, what would the pilgrimage look like *with* Beth? Round and round it went, one thought swirling into the next.

Eventually all the pieces fell into place and our group of five emerged. A week before we were due to depart for Spain, Sascha,

Meredith, Jess, Beth, and I gathered for dinner in the faculty apartment of the freshman dormitory to which I had been assigned. Every detail of our itinerary was reviewed one last time. We confirmed the arrival locations of our various flights, checked the expiration dates on our passports, and discussed which of the local banks we'd discovered would exchange dollars for Euros. Securing pocket change, as it turned out, would be the least of our worries.

Each member of the team also brought what they considered to be their essential pieces of equipment, including backpacks, sleeping bags, footwear, and raingear. Knowing the benefits of traveling light, we spent a number of hours inspecting these items, consolidating wherever possible.

This would prove a more difficult task than I first anticipated. A few months prior, Beth and I had ventured to our local REI store to make our two most important purchases – backpacks and hiking shoes. After much conversation with the sales staff, we settled on CamelBak® packs, specifically designed for a woman's smaller frame. Compact and lightweight, the packs came with a built-in hydration bladder we promptly nicknamed "the otter." Extending from the top of this water satchel was an over-the-shoulder drinking tube. Once the pack was on, the attached mouthpiece of the tube came to rest just beneath our clavicles. It was a brilliant design, allowing for constant access to water without the burden of carrying a bottle by hand.

Unfortunately, the towering pile of clothes and supplies scattered across my dining room floor completely dwarfed my new pack. Anticipating the trip would likely require spending 40 days outside, I had amassed gear for every possible scenario. Much of the stash came from shopping trips Beth had taken to our local Salvation Army store, a treasure trove of cheap clothing. But buying in bulk had backfired. Our coffer was now overflowing.

In addition to the requisite pairs of underwear, bras, socks, trail pants, and long sleeve t-shirts, I had thrown in a pair of gloves, a woolen hat and scarf, a rain poncho, a jacket, and a couple of fleece pullovers. Then there were the items I would need when I was off the trail: pajamas, shorts, a spare t-shirt, flip flops for the communal showers stalls that awaited me, a towel, an assortment of eyeglasses and, of course, something to read. That was non-negotiable.

Similarly, I couldn't imagine going on the pilgrimage without a baseball cap to keep the sun off my face. A faded Red Sox hat, tattered brim and all, was tossed in for good measure. A bandana and jackknife, some duct tape, and a camera, cell phone, and charger also found their way into the expanding heap. My toiletry bag was overflowing with every medicinal antidote known to mankind – everything from aspirin to tampons, band-aids to snake bite kits. Completing this array were my toothbrush, toothpaste, soap, shampoo, razors, deodorant, dental floss, hairbrush, tweezers, Vaseline, moisturizer, sunblock, Q-tips, antiseptic cream, ace bandages and, finally, a slew of pills to resolve anticipated bouts of diarrhea, constipation, headaches, and whatever else might ail me.

On the perimeter of this swelling stack were a pair of walking poles, binoculars, my passport, a pile of cash, airline tickets, a diary and pen, my wallet, the required pilgrim *Compostela*, a flashlight, a roll of toilet paper, my pillow, and a sleeping bag and mat. As I looked at the jumble spread out in every direction, I thought, *where am I going to pack my granola bars?*

This collection needed more than a weight loss plan. It needed a full-blown intervention.

Significant variations in climate forced me to reimagine using each garment for multiple purposes. I started with the clothes first. The scarf and jacket were out. If it was cold, I would simply walk faster. My extra pair of socks would double as gloves. Every other piece of clothing in the pile, with the exception of underwear and socks, would be reduced to a single item. One pair of pants, one t-shirt, one pair of shorts and so on down the line. Pajamas were deemed unnecessary. I would sleep in a t-shirt. I decided to use a facecloth as a towel, and then jettisoned the flashlight, toilet paper, sleeping mat, and binoculars. I took a pillowcase rather than the pillow. I could always stuff it with my fleece if I needed a soft landing place for my weary head. The extra pair of shoes was then discarded along with most of the items in my toiletry bag. In time, the mound became significantly slimmer, giving me at least a fighting chance at wedging the remaining items into my pack.

There were a number of things we decided to split between the five of us. After some discussion, we determined I would bring the medical supplies for the team. As the only man, Sascha was selected to carry the spare food supplies, a particularly weighty assignment. Meredith and Jess were planning to bring larger packs and offered to carry extra pieces of clothing. We slowly parsed our reservoir of supplies to the bare minimum, distributing the weight amongst the group.

Then came the cruelest cut of all. We decided, as a group, we would each take one "luxury" item on the trip, something that gave us pleasure or comfort, even if it wasn't practical. Beth and Meredith selected the same trinket, their iPods. Having music, both on the airplane and while walking, rocketed to the top of their wish list. Sascha, true to form, chose to bring a journal. It would help him remember the journey's highlights while also giving him a way to process what he was experiencing. Despite the added weight, Jess opted to bring both a large camera and a number of lenses. Always the artist, she couldn't make sense of such an adventure without the ability to capture it on film.

When it was my turn, I was torn. There are few things in the world that give me more pleasure than books. The thought of enduring two long flights, countless hours in various airports, and potentially 40 nights in rural Spain without something to read was virtually unthinkable. But books are heavy and my pack was already bulging. I also couldn't imagine leaving a book behind after I'd finished it. Creamy white pages filled with text feel more like friends to me than mere objects. Discarding such treasures didn't come easily. But toting them for the entirety of the pilgrimage made even less sense. Reluctantly, I pushed aside the bank of books I had selected and instead slipped 40 pieces of Bazooka bubble gum into the remaining side pocket of my pack.

Every day I was on the Camino, as the sun disappeared behind the horizon, I opened a piece of gum and popped it into my mouth. The gushing sweetness of it was heavenly. Although the burst of flavor didn't last for long, the promise of that sugary taste of home gave me something to look forward to, especially after a long or difficult day. My pack slowly grew lighter as my bubble gum supply dwindled. Later on, I would track my progress by counting how many pieces remained in that pocket. It was as if the trail had morphed into a giant Candy Land boardwalk, with each piece of gum bringing me one step closer to the finish line.

As we neared the end of our strategy session, I had just one last topic I wanted to discuss with the group. I thought it might be fun to choose nicknames for the trip; names that spoke to why each of us had agreed to embark on such a difficult journey. Given this would be a walking excursion, I suggested all of our monikers be a riff on the word "go."

I started. Without much thought, I blurted out, "Let Go." I am many things, but carefree is not one of them. For as long as I can remember I have held the reins a bit too tightly, guarding against unpredictable outcomes through ridiculous amounts of forethought and preparation. I am careful about what I say, emotionally level, and rarely do something I'll later regret. In the world of adults, these characteristics prove quite useful. These same traits translate into my being politically savvy, punctual, and well-behaved. I am often lauded as an ideal employee, a dedicated daughter, and a good and dependable citizen of the communities to which I belong.

But these proclivities also mean my stomach is frequently in knots. I regularly swallow damaging doses of emotional venom. I bite my tongue. I hold grudges. Little by little, all of this toxicity has created walls that I find nearly impossible to scale. While I am cordial on the outside, I am simultaneously guarded, remaining just out of arms' reach to almost everyone in my orbit. Even those I love.

I have become a master of conversational deflection, re-directing dialogue if it feels like it might hit too close to home. Sadly, most folks don't even notice this nuance, as friendly banter passes for intimacy far too easily these days.

But where these strategies have become most problematic are in situations that require my leadership. In moments where most people dictate, I build bridges, coaxing rather than directing. I rely far too frequently on persuasion and far too little on authority. And I resent it.

I have become a disciple of the Church of High Achievement. With a clergy collar, a Harvard degree, and a job at one of the preeminent schools in the nation, I have an enormous amount of credentialing. And yet, even as my intestines burn in revolt, I too often choose to behave, hamstrung by the golden handcuffs of popular opinion and financial security. Could the Camino be capable of breaking the bars of this self-imposed cage? Would walking 500 miles, filled with situations I could not control, literally beat the composure right out of me?

I sure hoped so.

Turning to my left, I looked to Beth to continue the "name game." Without missing a beat, she rolled her eyes and said with a certain wry exasperation, "Okay then, I'll be '*Just* Go'!" We all burst into laughter. She had hit the nail on the head. Throughout our previous discussions, Beth had been crystal clear about her intentions for the trip. She didn't like to walk, at least not if there wasn't an imminent destination in mind. She also loathed the heat, consistently complaining her feet were hot even in the dead of winter. And she wasn't crazy about the idea of sleeping in primitive shelters either, cozying up to a different cadre of strangers each night, with precious little privacy. She could appreciate the Camino on some kind of esoteric level, as a test of will or faith. But did that *really* necessitate 40 days of walking with only a handful of toilet paper to keep her dignity intact? She didn't think so. And frankly, it was hard to disagree with her.

But what Beth did realize was that the Camino was speaking *to me*, like one of those sirens from Homer's *Odyssey*, luring me toward a rocky and dangerous shore. I think she knew I was capable of finishing the pilgrimage, despite its difficulties. It's one of the traits I love most about her, that she believes in me, convinced I can outthink or outlast almost anything. At times I can actually feel the admiration beam from her eyes. It's enough to make my knees weak. What does she see that sparks such love and devotion? Truthfully, I'm not sure. But whatever it is, it was enough to get her to board a plane and set off on this adventure. She decided to "just go" because she had long ago committed to go with me no matter where the path led. Like the story of Ruth and Naomi, we were fused together on this journey of ours. Whether deserved or not, to be loved with that kind of wild abandon has been one of the greatest joys of my life.

I had met Sascha just two years prior, on the first day of his orientation to Phillips Andover, a prestigious boarding school located 20 miles or so northwest of Boston. Founded in 1778, Phillips remains the oldest incorporated academy in the nation, long a place of privilege and pedigree. Think blue blazers and regimental ties, attire befitting the captains of industry they were destined to be. Andover was "old school" for most of its illustrious history, filled with gentlemen's "C's" and future Yale alumni.

But then the 1970s arrived. Along with a tapestry that included the cultural schisms of Vietnam and Watergate, so too came women. In 1974, Andover granted diplomas for the first time to female graduates. It would be a watershed moment for the institution, although not one that was universally approved of or applauded. Now, nearly 50 years later, "PA" is a remarkably different place. A need-blind admissions policy has ensured access to the brightest of candidates, regardless of financial circumstance, station, or legacy. The institution has become quite intentional in its desire to craft a global community, a crucible capable of withstanding a wide variety of opinions and divergent perspectives. While Andover is still rooted in its blue-blood tradition, it functions far more these days like a web than a ladder.

I came to the school in the autumn of 2008, as their inaugural Director of Spiritual and Religious Life. At a time when many regarded religious leaders, and particularly Christians, as rabid proponents of a right-to-life, stem-cell bashing, evolution-denying, "love the sinner, hate the sin" heterosexual agenda, I was an unusual choice. Andover had taken more than 200 years to reassess its commitment to the spiritual development of its charges. Church attendance was not exactly running at an all-time high in those days, and it was a particularly unpopular activity for most adolescents. So why the investment? Why allocate more time and energy to this seemingly doomed institutional dinosaur?

Which begged another question. Why *me*? I had been ordained for less than five years at that point. Perhaps more striking, I was also female, a lesbian, and had a wife in tow. Surely that unholy combination should have been enough to sink my candidacy. But there I was, on the steps of the chapel that beautiful September day, when a 16-year-old Kansas farm boy bounded up the wide granite steps.

Affable, grinning, and with a deliciously silky baritone voice, there was just something about him. I was instantly taken by his Midwestern charm. He was a handsome kid, still growing into his shoulders. Now, just two years later, he sat on the couch across from me, pondering a suitable nickname for this most unusual of journeys.

Contemplation came naturally to him, and after a minute or so he confidently said, "Go Slow." We all nodded silently in agreement, for Sascha was frenetic about almost everything he did. He spoke with a hurried intensity. His mind didn't wander, it whirred. He often bounced his leg while sitting, constantly in a state of motion, even if it meant he was just going around in circles. It would be difficult for Sascha to let the wisdom of the Camino seep into his pores. He was much more liable to treat the trail as an obstacle to be conquered. A cross-country runner and marathoner, he already had the mental and physical toughness the pilgrimage would require. But he was also smart enough to know that his natural inclination to gallop over the Camino's brittle crust would obliterate its subtleties. He needed a scalpel, not a chain saw, to dissect this complicated campaign. Slowing down would be a good first step toward reaching that goal.

Originally, I had been wary of taking students on the trip. I knew the pilgrimage would be an ambitious undertaking. It would require all of my emotional strength, all of my coping skills, and all of my energy. With so little left to spare, I feared I wouldn't be able to take care of someone else. Care *for* them, yes. But not take care *of* them.

Ironically enough, I chose Sascha to come to Spain for the opposite reason – to take care of *me*. One night while walking back to the dorm after Sunday services, we were chatting about my interest in walking the Camino. He knew I was concerned about the physicality of the trek, an apprehension that was now keeping me up at night. Jokingly I said to him, "If you were to carry my pack on the trip, I'd give you a thousand dollars." His head quickly spun toward mine, and with the most plaintive of expressions he said, "I'll do it, Rev." Caught off-guard, I dismissed his chivalrous offer posthaste. I was kidding of course. But Sascha was not. "Seriously Rev, I'll carry your bag for you." I felt a catch in my throat. His proposal might have been impulsive but it was also so blatantly earnest it made my heart ache. He was 30 years younger, much stronger, and far more agile than I. Perhaps it wouldn't be such a bad idea to have a companion on the Camino like Sascha. "Let's *do* it!" I declared. Our pilgrimage family now numbered three.

Having just broken my "no student" rule, I began to ponder whether there might be others I'd like to invite. After conferring with Beth, I approached Meredith who, like Sascha, was due to graduate that spring. Mature and self-reliant, she was a natural choice. She had long ago earned our trust, our admiration, and our affection. Perhaps most importantly, she was curious about a wide variety of cultures and religions. Despite the Camino's Catholic origins, I thought Meredith might find the experience worth considering.

From a nearby wealthy town, Meredith had acclimated to her white, Christian neighborhood with little fanfare. She was the antithesis of what one would expect of a child of means. She was modest in every way; modest in dress, modest in demeanor, and unfailingly demure about her vast experiences traveling abroad and her accomplished academic record. Poised and polite, she wasn't a child pretending to be an adult. She actually was an adult, which is precisely how Meredith came to be part of our burgeoning posse.

During my first year at Phillips, I had more conversations of substance with Meredith than with any other student on campus. She had been assigned to work as a prefect in my dorm, a position given to a select group of upperclassmen deemed capable of helping oversee the residence halls on campus. Meredith, then an 11th-grader, was placed in a ninth-grade dorm to serve as an "older sister," as it were: there to help shepherd the youngest of our students during their often tumultuous first year.

I was assigned to cover the dorm one night a week. It was a task that required me to know the girls' whereabouts, supervise their studies, and make sure everyone was in bed by 11:00 p.m. As a junior in high school, Meredith wasn't required to adhere to these same rules, which meant she was free to spend her early evening hours with me, chatting about religion, politics, the *Twilight* series, her frequent travels to Pakistan, or something she had recently discovered on YouTube. As the first semester progressed, I began to look forward to our visits, intrigued by both her opinions and perspectives. But more than that, I enjoyed her company. She was smart, and sweet, and endearing in a way that many teenage girls are not. She was also wise beyond her years. Meredith was going to be a woman of importance someday, thoughtful and kind in a world desperately in need of both.

When it came time for her to select a nickname, she didn't hesitate. "Ami-go," she stated knowingly. She too had captured what would be the essence of her time on the trail. Although our youngest and shiest member, a Muslim on a historically Christian journey, Meredith would act as our group's envoy. Her facility with both French and Spanish would prove invaluable as the rest of us often found ourselves in need of her linguistic skill. Meredith would be our bridge, a friend to all, an "amigo" to those who came our way.

Four down, one to go.

All eyes now fell on Jess, the final piece of our Camino puzzle. We had become friends while working together some years back, bonded by the shared conviction that our then place of employment was the most dysfunctional in which we had ever worked. Jess was one of the few highlights of that experience for me, and if she were the only thing I would take from those years of misery, that would have been enough. More recently, she had been working as an art instructor at a nearby Catholic high school. It was meaningful work, a reality that unfortunately didn't seem to translate to her weekly paystub. She didn't have much cash but she *did* have time, a far more important commodity when it came to traversing the Camino.

She also had a zany sense of humor and an extraordinary amount of energy. She laughed easily and often. In her spare time, she taught a spin class and she had the body to show for it. Jess was hyper fit and just 29 years old. She would have no trouble walking the Camino. In fact, while the rest of us were mercurial in our quest to shrink our packs, Jess threw caution to the wind and supplemented her enormous camera with a smattering of makeup supplies. After all, what self-respecting woman would go on a trip without mascara?

I approached Jess about joining us on the pilgrimage because she was fun. Loads of fun. Side-splitting fun. The only real snag for her would be the cost. The pilgrimage itself is not an expensive endeavor. The hostels are modestly priced and some are even willing to accept a small donation in return for accommodation. The budget for food is also surprisingly low as most pilgrims eat very little during the day, their appetites naturally depressed by the combination of heat and exercise. What makes the Camino a potentially expensive adventure are the upfront costs – namely equipment and transportation. Thankfully, Jess already had much of the gear she would need, but the airfare was significant. After spending a few days searching the internet, she finally found a roundtrip ticket she could afford. Our team was now complete.

With a typically enthusiastic yelp, Jess hollered, "I'll be Go-GO!" An image of Nancy Sinatra, decked out in her signature white go-go boots, flashed through my mind. And so it was. Jess would be our trailblazer, our fitness guru, and our cheerleader, scooting across the terrain with her cascade of crazy blonde curls leading the way.

Later on, when we would meet other pilgrims along the way, they would inevitably ask how we all came to know each other. Were we friends? Not really. Did we meet on the Camino? Um, no. Family then? That was always the hardest to answer. Of a sort, I suppose. It wasn't like I didn't have time to explain the complicated latticework that bonded us. We were walking across Spain after all. But it always sounded a bit like one of those canned bar jokes.

"So a priest, a lesbian, a Muslim, a farmhand from Kansas, and a 29-year-old virgin walk into a bar…"

Wrapped Around My Finger

"I have only come here seeking knowledge,
Things they would not teach me of in college
I can see the destiny you sold
Turned into a shining band of gold."

—Sting, *Wrapped Around Your Finger*

Just before I left for the airport, I took off my wedding ring. I didn't want to leave it behind but I couldn't take a chance something would happen to it while I was hiking the Camino. I placed it gently down on the bedside table, turned, and exited the room.

I own precious few things to which I harbor any real attachment. But my wedding ring inspires a fierce, almost instinctual, allegiance. It's the embodiment of that which I hold most dear, which is why the thought of losing it inspired such dread. As I slipped it from my finger, it felt as if a protective force field had suddenly disappeared. The image of Wonder Woman popped into my head. Arms crossed in front of her chest, wielding her bracelets like shields, warding off errant bullets with a mere flick of a wrist. But I had no such armament without my ring, real or imagined. Only a circle of moist white skin, a tattoo of my new-found vulnerability.

The first time I got married, I used my maternal grandmother's ring, a simple gold band purchased at one of Boston's most venerable jewelers, Shreve, Crump, & Lowe. It always amused me that my grandmother, a domestic serving Commonwealth Avenue's upper crust, insisted her ring be purchased in Boston's swanky Back Bay. As it turned out, that ring, along with her penchant for beautiful hats, was her only vanity. A gleaming band for a hand coarsened by mopping floors and diapering babies.

That same ring was placed on my hand when I was in my mid-20s, released from the top drawer of my mother's dresser after patiently awaiting its "second act." I was never a diamond ring kind of gal, content with an ordinary band to mark my upcoming nuptials. Having my grandmother's ring was more than enough for me.

I met my soon-to-be husband during our freshman year in college. Although we both had ventured many hours from home, he hailed from the town adjacent to my own. He was off-the-charts smart, an engineer and physicist in the making. He was handsome, with the lean build of a cross country runner. He sported a cheesy mustache that was the envy of many of the baby-faced men in our entering class. Most importantly, he was kind, and gentle, and tender-hearted. He was a good man, in the purest sense of the word. I counted myself lucky to marry someone I knew loved me deeply and on whom I could rely. A good husband, a good partner and, hopefully someday, a good father.

The years rolled by in typical fashion. After we married, I moved to upstate New York where he was finishing his doctoral degree. With PhD in hand, he found a job in the aerospace industry, necessitating another bevy of moves. We eventually landed back in Boston, surrounded by the archetypal trappings of life in the suburbs.

While he spent his days designing telescopes to scan the heavens, I was meeting some dazzling comets of my own. As part of Harvard University's admission team, we were a magnet for the best and the brightest, the well-connected and the well-off. It was a plum job. We were comfortable. Everything seemed to be chugging along nicely.

We had married just a few days after Christmas, forever blending our anniversary date with the most frantic of holidays. We developed a number of rituals over time to mark both occasions, including designing and making our own Christmas cards each year. While lovely, this tradition added stress to December's already burdensome calendar.

After 11 years of marriage, almost to the day, we returned home after spending the day traveling back and forth between our families' various holiday gatherings. I was exhausted and made my way up the stairs for a late afternoon nap. Despite my fatigue, I couldn't sleep. I was agitated and restless, but I didn't know why. Frustrated, I got up, put on a sweatshirt, and came back downstairs. My husband met me in the kitchen and said casually, "We need to finish up our Christmas cards. We don't want to send them out too late." I watched as he turned, opened the refrigerator door, and peered inside.

"I can't," I answered.

Confused, he turned back toward me. "Honestly, we need to finish them," he lightly prodded.

"I can't," I whispered. "I just can't."

Robotically I spun and left the kitchen. I climbed the stairs, slowly and methodically. When I crossed the threshold into our bedroom it seemed oddly foreign to me, as if I no longer belonged there. Angling toward my closet, I slipped a few pieces of clothing into a small knapsack and put on my coat. When I came back down a few minutes later, my husband was still in the kitchen, frozen in place. He stood uneasily on the cold linoleum, searching my face for a clue as to what had just transpired.

I reached for my wallet, took out our joint bank and credit cards from the inside fold, and slid them onto the kitchen counter. "What are you *doing?*" he asked warily. I could see he was confused. But now he was afraid as well.

What *was* I doing? My mind went blank. I could hear my heartbeat in my ears, whoosh, whoosh, whoosh. My legs were rigid, locked at the knee. My eyes strangely dry. It occurred to me I had *no idea* what I was doing, or where I was going, or even what I was thinking. I was like the Tin Man from Oz, an empty shell devoid of emotion.

Staring straight ahead, I heard myself say, "I just … can't."

I plucked my car keys off the counter and wordlessly opened the door, stepped out into the frigid air, put the car in reverse, and headed into the darkness.

A few weeks later, I drove to my parents' house to tell them I had left my husband. It was a conversation I loathed to have, but that didn't make it any less necessary. I had put it off, partly because I couldn't explain what had happened, even to myself. All these years later, he was *still* a good man. Faithful, reliable, responsible. And I loved him but … But *what?* That was the question, I suppose. Still, the time had come to be honest about what was happening, even if it didn't make any sense.

When I arrived, my parents were sitting in a small room off the kitchen. It had been a porch when I was a child, and despite its long-ago renovation, was still referred to as the breezeway. Sunny and warm, it was where they spent most of their time, nestled into the corner of two small couches, each flanked by side tables that held a teetering pile of necessities. For my Mom; her coffee cup, a phone, a handful of No. 2 pencils for the daily newspaper crossword puzzle, a stack of books, and the television remote. For my Dad; his reading glasses, some old radio magazines, a police scanner, and a cannister of faux fish treats for the cat.

They were a bit surprised to see me, a visit unprompted by a request for an errand or chore to be done. Eying the available seats, I claimed the remaining space on the couch on which my father had plopped, turning slightly askew so I could face both. Without too much of a preamble, I told them I had left my marriage and was living in a small studio apartment near my office. I quickly explained the decision had been mine and that my husband had neither said nor done anything to warrant what seemed to be a hasty and drastic decision.

Like a vice grip, a deadening silence clamped down over the room. I glanced at my father first. His palms were resting on top of his thighs. He looked straight ahead, seemingly transfixed by the swirling design of the room's 1970s wallpaper. All of the color had drained from his face.

He is frightened, I remember thinking, scared of what might happen to me now that I was alone. Slowly he trained his eyes toward my mother, as if to plead, *do something, say something* that will make all of this go away.

I turned next to my mother, waiting for the onslaught to begin. She was never one to hold her tongue and I braced myself for the surge I was certain was to follow. But her face was placid, waxlike in its stillness. And then she uttered four words, four words that instantly crystallized the years of angst that had been fermenting in the dark recesses of my heart.

"I saw you ... shrinking."

Tears sprang from the corner of my eyes. I didn't say anything else. Neither did she.

In the days, weeks, and months that followed, she never second-guessed me. She never asked me if I was sure I was doing the right thing. Or if I had thought it all through. She trusted my decision was not capricious or cavalier but essential *to my survival.* All those years, when I thought she didn't see me, when I thought she might not even be paying attention, she was watching.

She knew. She always knew, even when I didn't.

When I look back on that fateful Christmas day, I know my leaving was not rooted in some sort of selfishness or manipulation. I wasn't trying to hurt my husband, although I certainly did; something that pains me even now. What happened that day was an act of desperation. I was bleeding to death from paper cuts, rivulets that drained my spirit so surreptitiously I had scarcely even noticed.

I walked into that bitter December night gasping for the pocket of air that would save me from drowning. How had I possibly held my breath for so long?

Strikingly, that decision still haunts me. Not because my marriage ended, but because it started. Just a few hours before I was to be wed, my father came and rapped on the door of my childhood bedroom. I was nearly ready. My hair was coiffed and some mascara applied. My dress hung on the back of the closet door, at the ready. He was wearing a black tuxedo, shoes shined and smelling of Old Spice aftershave. I waved him in and he stood next to me, smiling so broadly his eyes crinkled.

I assumed he had come to check on me and we swapped a bit of small talk. Just before leaving, he paused at the door, turning his face toward mine. "Are you sure?" The question was proffered so softly, so gently, it hung in the air between us like mist.

I batted it away with a quick grin, assuring him I was just fine. His eyes softened. Then he nodded, smiled, and pulled the door closed behind him.

On more than one occasion I have replayed that moment in my head. I have wondered what my life would look like if I had paused, if I had chosen another path, perhaps the journey my father saw as my future. Years later my husband would remarry, become a father, seemingly happy with the new life he created. And yet, I still consider the end of my marriage to be my biggest failure. Sins of omission, things you don't say or don't do, are often the most damaging.

My grandmother's ring became a source of shame for me, a symbol of a promise broken. When it came right down to it, she had a much harder row to hoe than I. An immigrant from Ireland in the early 1900s, she was *persona non grata* in a town that would gain notoriety for class strife and racial segregation. NINA (No Irish Need Apply) signs blanketed nearly every block during that era. The disdain for this newest wave of arrivals was palpable. The Irish who populated the gritty alleys of South Boston were largely known for their boorish behavior and proclivity for drinking. Just a teen herself, my grandmother had no use for such nonsense. She married a soft-spoken teetotaler who, like her, had emigrated from Galway. Although my grandfather worked as a manual laborer with the railroad, he and my grandmother scraped together the funds needed to move away from the city and into a small farmhouse where they raised children and chickens and, in my grandmother's case, raised hell.

Her spirited temperament made her a neighborhood favorite. Quick-witted and sharp-tongued, she was the life of the party back in the day. But it wasn't all roses. She lost a child to scarlet fever. Another was struck by a train and killed. Although she reared four others to adulthood – a doctor, a chemist, a priest, and a nurse – she never truly recovered from those earlier losses.

Still, she kept on living. She kept on moving, even if at times she was just going through the motions. Every night she laundered her husband's shirts by hand in an old basin balanced on top of the kitchen stove. She whitewashed the picket fence when the weather grew warm enough. She chased the neighborhood drunks off her property with a frying pan held shoulder-high. She was a working woman who made her living by virtue of having a strong back and a stronger will.

But that delicate golden band, the one that cut so tightly into her meaty paws in her later years, didn't deter her from chasing bigger dreams. It was a sign of where she was headed, a shining arc of hope that her immigrant roots and chafed hands would not define her.

In many ways, I am the benefactor of my grandmother's dedication and hard work. All those years of menial labor bred in her a thirst for accomplishment and success, a mindset inherited by my mother, and later by me. It saddens me to know the ring my grandmother wore all of her adult life, I took off. And in doing so, I broke the only tangible link that remained between us.

Many years later, when I decided to remarry, I was determined no such legacy would be attached to my next wedding band. It would be fresh and new, crafted to reflect my latest chance at love. After much conversation, Beth and I decided our rings would be comprised of a single swath of yellow gold, bordered on each side by two narrow strips of platinum. The plain center band was an homage to my first ring. The two outer loops represented the two external supports every good marriage needs – family and friends. The design beautifully captured the tone Beth and I wanted. But when we went to retrieve our newly minted creations, something wasn't right.

They were just so … *shiny*.

I asked the jeweler if he could roughen the surface of the middle band, scratch it up somehow. He blanched. I persisted. After all, I was far too old for some gleaming new bauble. I wanted the ring to show I had accumulated a few dings along the way. Something that filled me with pride, not remorse. All of that history was part of me and would soon be part of my marriage. A flawless ring just didn't strike the right tone.

In the end, he did what I asked. And luckily, my marriage is none the worse for the wear. But on this particular day, as I prepared to set off for Spain, the memory of my ring would have to be enough. It was staying and I was going.

I bent over and kissed the smooth cotton pillowcase where Beth laid her head each night and then rumbled down the stairs of our apartment, headed to the airport and our next great adventure.

Lent

n. A period of penitence and fasting.

¡Bienvenido!

"And this is precisely the secret held by all those who go by foot: life is prolonged when you walk. Walking expands time rather than collapses it."

—Erling Kagge

While there are a number of paths to Santiago, the oldest and most established is the *Camino Francés*, the route that hugs the border between France and Spain. It begins in the village of St. Jean Pied-de-Port ("foot path" as the name translates), a dot that lies at the base of the Pyrenees mountains. It is from here that many pilgrims begin their 494.6-mile (796 km) trek to Santiago.

There is a certain cachet given to those who begin at St. Jean, not only because they walk the route in its entirety, but because the climb over the Pyrenees is exceedingly difficult. Many eager young legs wilt while traversing this pass, leaving a trail of blisters and pulled hamstrings in their wake. Given the challenges, I was stunned to learn how many Europeans actually walked *from their homes* to St. Jean, before proceeding on to the pilgrimage. Prior to the invention of modern transit, this was how every pilgrim found his or her way to St. Jean. Thankfully, my home was separated from Spain by a vast ocean, rendering this scenario impossible. Bullet dodged.

Our group made the decision to begin our journey in Pamplona, a mid-sized city located 42 miles west of St. Jean. Pamplona houses a regional airport, providing all of us with a convenient way to reach our destination. While this meant we would miss a chunk of the original path, the plan was a good compromise. Finding our way to St. Jean would have required each of us to arrange for a bus or taxi to take us to the head of the trail after landing in Pamplona. We were all flying different airlines and arriving on different days. Given the logistical challenges already present, there was no need to further complicate our itinerary. Even so, I winced a bit when asked by other pilgrims where I began my journey, as if I had let an important badge of honor slip away.

Prior to our departure, Beth made a reservation for our crew at a place called Hostel Hemingway. Minutes away from a city bus stop and the famed Plaza del Castillo, it was a modestly priced venue we could all afford. Roughly 20 dollars per person would buy us breakfast, a shower, and a bunk bed. The hostel was centrally located and provided an ideal start line for our journey. From there we would be able to quickly get our bearings, cut through the heart of Pamplona, and intersect with the Camino as it made its way toward the outskirts of town.

Jess arrived first, a day ahead of everyone else, stopping for a layover in Portugal. She took a bus back to the airport the next day to meet Beth and me. It was a connection we almost missed. Our initial flight to New York's Kennedy airport had been delayed an hour. Our Iberia Air flight from New York to Madrid, another two hours. This shrunk our window to catch our last puddle-jumper to Pamplona to the smallest of slivers. As we headed up the aisle to exit the plane in Madrid, a particularly aggressive woman bumped Beth from behind. When she turned to speak to her, the woman squawked that she was late for her flight to Pamplona, as were her 14 guests! "Good," we exclaimed. "You seem to know where you're headed. We'll just follow you!" Sure enough, she peeled down the jet bridge and hooked a left at a small sign that read "Pamplona" in big block letters.

Something about our appearance must have been askew. Even so, after convincing a very circumspect airline employee we too were headed to Pamplona, we were whisked across the tarmac to a waiting plane. No one checked our tickets or our passports. Perhaps Spaniards were a bit more casual when it came to security? Hard to know. The flight was clearly going to Pamplona. We might as well get on.

By the time we found two open seats, we noticed the people around us had begun to stare. In our trail pants and hiking boots, we were wildly underdressed. Even if we were in the wrong place, it was too late now. Before we could think much more about it, the door closed and the plane began to make its way down the runway. As the head steward passed a particularly well-dressed man seated on the aisle in the front row, I heard him say, *"¡Bienvenido, Señor Presidente!"* While it was evident he wasn't *that* Mr. President, we definitely had taken a wrong turn. Somehow, we had been allowed to board a private plane. This explained why no one had asked for a boarding pass nor checked our bags. For the remainder of the flight, we slumped in our seats, eyes cast downward, hoping no one would notice the two scruffy vagabonds who had tagged along for the ride.

Upon reaching our destination, we exited the plane as quickly and graciously as we could. Jess was waiting for us in the terminal. We hugged, we squealed, and then we headed to Pamplona via the local shuttle bus. Sascha and Meredith had taken a third option, flying on Aer Lingus, a choice that allowed them time to order a Guinness or two during their layover in Dublin. It was Meredith's first alcoholic beverage ever. Her adventure was off to an auspicious start. Once on Spanish soil, they too found their way to the hostel. We had all made it safely. We were finally *in Spain*, just hours away from starting our pilgrimage.

Despite all the planning and conversation that had led up to this moment, being together in Pamplona still seemed surreal. Nestled in my bunk that night, I stole one last peek at the others before shutting my eyes. It was not a dream, I murmured under my breath. Tomorrow we would walk the Camino.

The author and Sascha, on the outskirts of Pamplona

Fatty

"We can't have our dear ones back, not as they were, not as we loved them. It isn't the beloved that resurrects. It's love itself."

—Kate Braestrup, *Marriage and Other Acts of Charity*

In retrospect, my dream of walking the Camino started with my parents' cat. Fatty, as we lovingly named her, was a skinny little thing. She was the runt of the litter with a coat of shiny, silky black fur. Closer in personality to a dog than a cat, she followed each of us around all day long, waiting for someone to find their way to the couch where she could snuggle up tight. She would happily remain there for hours, occasionally flipping over like a pancake to warm her opposing flank. Every now and then she would open those big green eyes of hers, blink laconically, and smile.

That cat. She was sweet as pie.

She politely accepted the affection I lavished upon her, but I always knew I wasn't her favorite. That reverence was reserved exclusively for my Dad. If he was standing at the sink, Fatty was at his heel. If he was working on the computer, she would sit beside the keyboard. Wherever he went, she followed.

This same routine played out with all of our childhood pets. First, my mother would push my father to allow the latest stray to join our clan. My Dad would say no. Then she would ignore his plea and make her way to the local shelter armed with enough cash for whatever shots or neutering were required. Afterwards she would lament her "free cat" was pretty pricey, but that never stopped her. Once she darkened the door of our neighborhood animal rescue facility, they had her at "hello."

By the time she came home with Fatty, my father had learned to just sigh and move on. Having been raised on a farm, he saw animals as a means to an end. Dogs were meant for herding. Cats for rodent control. Chickens, sheep, and cattle for food. But his post-World War II life in suburbia had weakened his resolve, and my mother knew it. "Complain all you want, Ted," she would say. "We're *getting* a cat."

One afternoon, as my father headed toward the kitchen, Fatty was following so closely she had to dart through his legs at the last second to avoid having her tail squashed under his heel. She managed to skitter away, but my Dad tumbled to the floor, landing with a large bang on the room's braided carpet. He had fallen numerous times over the years and had perfected the "tuck and roll" maneuver needed to avert injury. This day was no exception.

Having come to a stop just shy of the kitchen table, he hollered to my mother, seated in the next room, that he was all right. But at 87 years old, he was going to need some assistance returning to vertical.

My mother, then 78, crossed through the kitchen and attempted to help him regain his footing. After a lifetime of relying exclusively on his arms to lift himself out of various chairs and couches, his chest was taut with muscle. And yet there was no angle, no position he could find that would allow him to push himself back up. Finally, seeing no other option, they agreed my mother should call 911 and have the ambulance personnel hoist him to his feet.

She lifted the receiver of the old rotary phone still hanging on the kitchen wall and began to dial. "No rush," she told the operator. "He's fine. We just need a bit of help righting the ship." After a few minutes, the ambulance arrived. Two paramedics hopped up the porch stairs and into my parents' house. Looping their arms underneath his, they quickly brought my Dad back to his full and upright position.

"Thanks boys. I sure do appreciate it," he said, reaching out to shake their hands.

"I'm sorry sir," the driver answered sheepishly, "but you need to come with us. Whenever we respond to a call, we are required to bring the patient to the hospital for a complete check."

"That won't be necessary. I'm fine," my father demurred.

"I'm sorry sir. It's protocol," came the response.

Glancing at my mother, he shrugged. "Well, okay then. Let me get my jacket." Soon enough he was headed down the driveway, followed by both EMTs. He assured my mother he would return shortly. She had given up driving a few years prior and told him she'd find someone to bring him home after his exam was complete. With a plan in place, he slipped into the front seat of the ambulance and headed toward the hospital.

But he would not return. Not that day. Not any day. In less than 72 hours, my father died in that hospital. As I watched him take his last breath, I remember thinking nothing was ever going to be the same again.

Fleche Amarillo

"And yet I think there is a flood of beauty beyond the smoothness of youth; and my heart aches for that grace of longing that flows through bodies no longer straining to be innocent but yearning for redemption."

—Janet Morley, excerpt from *The Bodies of Grownups*

The province of Navarra is one of the many regions of Spain through which the Camino meanders. It's known for its rugged and mountainous terrain, as well as being a profitable breeding ground for horses, bulls, and trout. Pamplona is located on the western edge of this province, just before it gives way to the lush wine regions of La Rioja.

What little I knew about Pamplona had come from Hemingway novels and television coverage of the upcoming "running of the bulls," a quaint tradition that involves trying to outrun a stampede of what look to be very muscular and angry steers. The afternoon before we were to set out, Beth, Jess, and I took a walk through the town's narrow streets, including a stop at the famous bull ring. Tall wooden rails lined the street leading to its entrance, presumably to protect the crowd on the day of the event. Daring young men could leap over the fence at any point to test their mettle against the marauding mob of cattle. It all looked a bit grisly to me.

We rose early the next morning, bursting with excitement and adrenaline. After wolfing down some toast and a small glass of juice, I passed through the doorway and took the first official steps of our pilgrimage. Although the hostel was located near the old city and close to the bull ring, it was not actually on the Camino. Which meant our first order of business would be to find our way out of the neighborhood and on to the pilgrimage path. The day prior, I had purchased a map for this very reason, a detailed grid of every street and every square. I sketched a route from the hostel to the closest junction of the Camino, zigzagging our way through town. As we headed west, we kept an eye out for the image of a scallop shell or *fleche amarillo* (yellow arrow), both used to mark the pilgrimage route. Our scavenger hunt had begun.

We discovered our first sign in less than 20 minutes. It was a blue and yellow shell tacked high atop the telephone pole of a nearby intersection. We let out a collective yelp as we came upon it, relieved to have located the famed path. Brimming with exuberance, we asked a crossing guard to take a photograph of us underneath the sign. She granted the request before whisking us off the corner and across the street. Of the countless pictures I have of our trip, that photo is among my favorites. When I look it now, all I see is how our faces glowed with anticipation. We were having a ball.

Once outside the city limits, we began the steep ascent leading to the top of Alto del Perdón (Hill of Forgiveness). The climb reached an altitude of 2,590 feet (789 m), making my lungs heave with exertion. Despite my best effort to minimize, my pack still seemed unduly heavy. My shoulders ached with the strain. While trying to navigate the large loose stones that covered the path, I slowed to a near crawl. The rush of adrenaline I felt earlier had evaporated.

But fatigue didn't stop me from being completely gobsmacked by my surroundings. I was mesmerized by the scenery. Mile after mile after mile I bisected wavy fields of tall grass, the greenish-gold stems glistening in the sunlight. As the profile of Pamplona began to shrink in the distance, a string of white windmills appeared. Their blades spun furiously, emitting a soft hum, the only audible sound. Awash in a landscape of amber and blue, I was ringed by beautiful vistas at every turn.

By midday we reached the crest on which the windmills were perched. We were a bit lethargic by that point, but determined to press on. We stopped briefly to marvel at a string of metal sculptures decorating the hill's apex. The stationary figures all faced west, eyes fixed on the horizon. Following their lead, we headed in the same direction, gingerly making our way down the backside of the hill's spine until we reached the small settlement of Uterga.

Metal sculptures atop Alto del Perdón

Jess must have taken a hundred pictures that day. But the one image of our inaugural jaunt that sticks in my mind is of Beth. Those first 10 miles were much more arduous than anything she had done in her abbreviated training regimen. Whenever I caught sight of her that day, her head was down, her face drained and drawn with strain. Still, she never complained. Not once.

When we stopped mid-morning to sit on a bench tucked under the cooling shade of a tree, Beth finally had a chance to take in the landscape. She looked out at the panorama before her in utter wonder. Watching her in that moment made my heart swell; partly with pride and partly in appreciation for the extraordinary gift she had given me. She had ventured to Spain only because I had asked her. It was an act of enormous generosity and love. Many years earlier, for our wedding ceremony, we had chosen a passage from the Hebrew scriptures that extolled the fierceness with which Ruth bound herself to Naomi, two women facing very difficult circumstances. At a crossroads, Ruth turns to Naomi and emphatically declares, "Do not press me to leave you or to turn back from following you. Where you go, I will go; where you lodge, I will lodge; your people will be my people and your God my God" (*New Revised Standard Version*, Ruth 1:16). Beth had made good on her vow, just as she had promised.

After meandering through a grove of almond trees, we rambled up to a hostel named Albergue Camino del Perdón. The word albergue is used to describe the simple accommodations available to those on the trail. To access these facilities, hikers must first show a credential, confirming their status as a pilgrim. Once the host reviews and stamps it, a bunk and shower can be had for minimal cost. The term albergue and hostel are often used interchangeably by those on the trail. No matter the nomenclature, I was thrilled to have found a place where we might be able to stay for the night.

This particular albergue boasted a stone terrace, a small restaurant, and five available beds. We were sold. Dropping our packs, we headed first for the showers before sitting down at the long wooden table located on the hostel's back patio. We were the only dinner guests that evening, and babbled excitedly about our day while inhaling every morsel on our plates. The Camino had already intoxicated us with its vistas and promises of adventure. We couldn't wait for day two.

I scribbled in my journal for 15 minutes or so, then haltingly lowered my weary body onto the bunk and closed my eyes. The thought that lingered wasn't the afternoon's stunning display of windmills or the slab of butter I had slathered on my bread during supper. It was of Alto de Perdón. Was it fate that something named the "Hill of Forgiveness" was the centerfold of my first day on the Camino? Was its appearance some kind of cosmic shot across the bow? If so, trouble was brewing.

Forgiveness, unfortunately, was not my strong suit.

45

"Not all who wander are lost."

—J.R.R. Tolkien, *The Fellowship of the Ring*

I had originally come to Spain thinking an extended hiatus would allow me time to take stock of my life. I had landed in Pamplona 50 days before my 50th birthday – a numerology that wasn't planned but likely wasn't coincidental either. I anticipated needing 40 days to walk to Santiago. It would be a Lenten ritual of a kind, and surely enough time to sort through the emotional ebb and flow that middle age inevitably brings.

No doubt some of those latent memories would be painful; the kind that most of us try to quash with frenetic social calendars, exhausting work commitments, excessive food and alcohol consumption, or compulsive exercising for the more health-conscious of us. But the Camino would strip me of all those coping mechanisms, leaving me to fend off the penetrating silence only miles of empty landscape can induce.

It would be here, in the remote hills and plateaus of Spain, that I would be free to let all those old tapes play in my head; feel them again, muse on their lessons and, hopefully, let them go. That was my prayer.

I was 45 when my father died. Too old to feel orphaned. Too young to feel ready. I was sitting at my desk at work when my mother called to tell me he had been taken to the hospital and was not expected to be released, as she had initially assumed. I hung up, ran down the stairs and jumped into my Honda, gunning for the hospital. As the scenery flew past, an uneasiness settled in my stomach. I knew my father wasn't sick. So why had they kept him?

After throwing the car in park, I hustled through the hospital's sliding doors and found my way to the counter in the reception area. I was told my father had been taken to a small private room just a few steps away from the central nursing station. He was in bed resting comfortably when I entered the room, flashing an easy smile.

"What are you doing here, Dad?" I queried.

"Beats me," he offered. "They said they wanted to take a look."

While we waited for the doctor to appear, he told me the story of how Fatty had caused him to fall, about the guys who had brought him in, then followed with a routine and gentle reminder to call my mother more often.

The assigned physician finally arrived, his affect professional and calm. No clues there. But then the words began, tumbling out in a confusing and nonsensical blur. What do you *mean* he has cancer? Everywhere? What do you mean *everywhere*? When I snatched a quick glance at my father's face, his attention was simultaneously focused and detached.

As if playing a recorded message, the doctor described the cancer that had invaded my father's chest, abdomen, and lungs. He continued with a perfunctory tutorial on radiation and chemotherapy. I felt the room begin to spin. A line of sweat began to bead on my forehead.

What are you *saying*? How could any of this *possibly* be true? Look at him. He's *fine*. Why are you still talking?

Meanwhile my father nodded silently, seemingly neither surprised nor concerned. At the end of his assessment, the doctor turned toward me and asked me to step outside into the hallway. My Dad motioned his consent. I got up and wobbled out into the corridor.

"You will need to convince him to seek treatment," he stated flatly. I returned this request with a blank stare. "I'm not sure he understands the severity of his condition. I recommend we begin the suggested protocol immediately." Turning on his heels, he headed toward the next room.

When I returned to my father's cubby, I edged my hip onto the side of his bed. "The doctor wants you to start chemotherapy," I began. But before I even got to the next sentence he reached out and, softly patting the top of my hand with his, gently shook his head. "But Dad," I stammered.

In a whispered but metered tone, his answer was definitive. "I'm not going to do that. I've had a good long run. Enough is enough."

I knew, right then and there, he wouldn't change his mind. He had reached the end of the road. He was done. Maybe he already knew he was sick. Maybe he didn't. What did it matter now anyway? The only thing left to do was to finish the way he wanted.

He politely declined to eat or drink from that moment on. Occasionally a respiratory therapist would stop by to suction the mucus that began to collect in his lungs; it was an unpleasant task for all involved. Without nourishment, he quickly grew weak. The nurses responded by quietly hanging a bag of morphine next to his bed, attaching the feed to an IV portal they had affixed to the top of his hand. Beth, my brother and his wife, her parents, and my favorite aunt held vigil at his bedside. While the others came and went, Beth, Aunt Mary, and I remained for the duration.

Without my father's oversight, my mother, an insulin-dependent diabetic, landed in the same hospital within 24 hours. They put her in a different room just down the hall. Throughout the day I bounced back and forth. My mother stabilized quickly with proper nutrition and medication. My father drifted in and out of sleep.

During what would be his final day, I asked my mother if she wanted the nurses to help her into a wheelchair so she could visit my father. Her response stung with ardor. "He doesn't want to see me. He wants to see *you*." I recoiled, as if absorbing a blow. While there may have been some truth to her assertation, I think her comment was largely her way of telling me she couldn't say goodbye to my father, not at his bedside, not on display.

That night, for the first time, my father seemed agitated, twisting in bed as if in pain. When the nurses finally checked, they noticed his morphine drip had gotten tangled, cutting off the flow of medication. As soon as they released the kink, a calm came over him. He opened his eyes briefly and called out my name. "I'm right here, Dad. It's okay. I'm right here."

My name would be the last word he would say.

When the others left for the night, the nurses offered scrubs to Beth, Mary, and me. It had been a long day and we were all feeling a bit grimy. I tiptoed into the bathroom, took off my clothes, and slipped the blue cotton uniform over my head. After splashing some warm water on my face, I crept back into the room. The air pulsed with the noise and gurgle of machines.

We dragged three big plastic chairs next to his bed. Laying across them, each of us tried to sleep, but to no avail. In the morning, my father's breathing seemed shallow and intermittent. Sensing the end was close, I made one final request. Could one of the nurses please give him a shave? As a career military man, he was maniacal about keeping his hair short and his whiskers shorn. Within a few minutes one of the staff came in and placed a hot towel on his face. A small dollop of shaving cream was gently swirled on to his cheeks and neck, followed by the smooth sharp strokes of a razor. Patting his freshly shaven face, I thought he looked as peaceful as I had ever seen him.

My brother and his in-laws returned in the wee hours of the morning, sitting quietly at the foot of the bed. When my brother left the room to go outside to smoke, my father's breathing grew more faint. Each time he inhaled, we waited to see if it would be his last. Soon enough it was.

My brother wasn't there for that final moment and neither was my mother. At first, I judged them for putting their own comfort before his. But over time I came to understand it wasn't that they wouldn't see him through to the end. It was that they *couldn't*.

My father's death, just a few short days after his admission to the hospital, shook me to my core. I was devastated.

And now, here I was on the Camino, just a touch shy of my 50th birthday. By then, the loss had seeped deeply into the marrow of my bones. But I hadn't yet come to terms with it, not really. I had come to Spain, in part, to exorcise that grief from my heart. I had come looking for peace.

What would have happened if Fatty hadn't tripped my father that day? How long would he have lingered while the cancer cells multiplied unabated? What if I hadn't had the chance to see him to the end, painful though it was?

I suppose these are part and parcel of life's mysteries. Perhaps the Camino would become my magic eight ball, offering insightful answers to my lingering questions. Time would tell.

Time was all I had left.

Chicago

"'Tis good to walk till blood appears on the cheek,
but not sweat on the brow."

—*Spanish proverb*

We called her Chicago. She was the first person we met on the Camino, a 70-something solo hiker from the Windy City with long flowing white hair gathered loosely in a ponytail. We had caught up to her at the end of our first day, standing next to the metal sculptures on Alto del Perdón. She exuded a no-nonsense kind of vibe. Over time, she let her guard down. But we had to earn it. I was cowed by her toughened exterior. Getting to know Chicago felt like breaking in the leather of a new baseball glove.

She was the first of many friends we made while on our pilgrimage. I've found walking lends itself to developing an easy banter with folks, particularly with new acquaintances. The awkward silences that crop up during face-to-face conversation are often avoided when walking side by side. Somehow the movement seems to grease the skids.

The natural cadence of these exchanges was helped significantly by the fact we were all going the same way, *literally* – a linear jaunt headed toward the great cathedral of Santiago. As each of us strolled along, other pilgrims would pass by, clipping along like race horses. But more often than not, a fellow traveler would linger, happy to stay in lockstep with us for a few minutes or even a few days.

I stand just over five feet tall, with a meager 28-inch inseam. There were precious few pilgrims whose stride stand as truncated as mine. In fact, it only took a couple of hours for our group of five to realize we weren't going to be able to hike together given the differences in age, height, body type, and fitness level. I was slow and deliberate, almost never adjusting my gait or speed despite the ever-changing terrain. Beth was fast going up hills but tentative going down. Meredith and Sascha, nearly the same height and age, walked comfortably together most days. And Jess, who we later dubbed "Panther," took the Camino by storm, churning up dust behind her no matter what the topography.

Given my choppy step, my interactions with other hikers on the trail were generally limited to brief vignettes. I would come upon someone sipping water while seated on a bench, someone bandaging a blister, or someone just splayed out on the grass resting. We would call out greetings. A piece of fruit might be swapped, or some snippet of information shared about the weather or the proximity of the next albergue. These encounters, while lovely, were short-lived. Soon enough my acquaintance would motor off, leaving me to scuff down the path on my own. Meeting Chicago was an unexpected treat. Although she was quite fit, her age had slowed her just enough to match my stride. I had met my Thelma. She had met her Louise.

Chicago joined our small tribe for the next few days, meandering in and out of cadence with the rest of us. We had spent our first day on the trail ascending Alto de Perdón, a climb made even more difficult by the scorching sun. It was a relief to begin day two walking through a series of lush vineyards cooled by a light drizzle of rain. Traversing the flat dirt path, we walked 4 miles before landing in Puente la Reine, our designated breakfast stop.

We bought some grapes, bananas, and a wedge of cheese from the local grocer as provisions for our afternoon snack, then headed to the town's only café. We sat down at the closest table to the door and tossed our packs in a heap against the back wall.

After placing our orders, I turned in my seat to scan the restaurant's décor. Oddly enough, the walls were covered with American sports memorabilia, including a statue of basketball great Michael Jordan, erroneously wearing number 32 (an inversion of his actual jersey number 23). Even in the rural outposts of Spain, American culture had managed to find a foothold.

By the time we cleaned our plates, sheets of rain had appeared on the other side of the restaurant's picture window. I fished out my poncho, poked my head through the neck hole, then draped my pack in plastic. Time to get wet.

As we made our way out of the village, the trail grew steep. The heavy downpour had turned the path's fine red clay into a slick of mud. We inched up the side of the hill, holding on to nearby branches and vegetation as we went, before making a careful descent on the far side of the ridge. Orienting our bodies parallel to the incline, we dug our heels into the waterlogged ground before lurching sideways, step over step, down the slippery slope.

Sascha lent me his walking stick in hopes of keeping me from skidding off the edge, a precarious and very real possibility. He had also changed out of his boots and into a pair of flip flops. While the rest of us weren't convinced this was the best tactic, at least he wasn't ruining his footwear. By the time we reached the bottom, we were all covered in mud.

The muddy feet of (left to right) Sascha, Beth, Jess,
and Meredith, outside of Mañeru

Cold, drenched, and weary, we opted to ditch our first plan and instead spent the night in Lorca, some 5 miles (8.4 km) short of Estrella, our original goal. Our disappointment didn't last for long. Who greeted us at the door of the 36-bed La Bodega del Camino? Chicago, of course. Welcoming us home.

16

Fountain of Wine

"Like a million cowards and trailblazers before me, I had
mistaken being gone for being free."

—Gail Caldwell, *A Strong West Wind*

I'm not sure if it was the change in altitude, the food, or the result
of significantly increased levels of exertion, but by day three my
stomach was in knots. The others waited patiently for me while
I hunkered in the bathroom. Their loitering, well-intentioned
though it might have been, only made my intestinal plight worse.

I soon realized there was more to my digestive distress
than just a change in routine. I was anxious. Anxious about
the responsibility of planning the day's route. Anxious about
whether the others were enjoying their experience. Anxious
about Beth's ability to meet the physical demands of the Camino.
Anxious about being in charge of everyone and everything.

I was obviously not making much headway with this "letting
go" thing.

But outside, the morning sun had begun to peek out, lifting
everyone's mood, including mine. The landscape was stunning.
Light bathed the stone buildings with a golden hue. Beautiful

puffy clouds stretched across the cerulean sky. As I strode down the trail, it was as if I were walking into a postcard.

Jess wanted to walk to Estrella at her own pace and had headed out early. Surprisingly enough, I matched her progress, mostly because she stopped so often to take photographs. When we both arrived at the edge of town, we paused to wait for the others. Beth straggled in. She had lost her buoyancy by that point and looked fragile and exhausted. This prompted another alteration to the plan. Sascha and Meredith would spend a few hours in Estrella, seeing the sites and having lunch, before finding us mid-afternoon. Beth, Jess, and I would continue to a small town just up the road and secure overnight accommodations. We had heard there was a "fountain of wine" located nearby. The promise of an endless spicket of cabernet lured us onward.

Chicago soon ambled up alongside us as we shuffled out of Estrella. We chatted a bit and then, just as we had been told, the fountain of wine appeared as if on cue. Less of a fountain and more of a faucet, we discovered a small lever attached to the side of a stone wall that provided a steady stream of red wine to parched pilgrims and would-be oenophiles. Beth and I tried a swig, but its bitter bite stunted our interest in a second glass. We had to chase Jess down as she had walked right past the fountain, tearing up the path in typical panther fashion.

We took a slew of pictures before noticing we were being filmed on the fountain's webcam. Every so often, even now, I still log on to the website to see if any pilgrims are toasting their progress. Once again, we were on our way.

After walking for a long stretch, I began to grow concerned when the hostel we had chosen didn't materialize. I stopped, retrieved the guidebook out of my pack, and realized I had confused the names of two of the towns. The landing spot we had chosen was still miles away. One look at Beth and I knew our plan needed to change for the second time that day.

Just around the corner was a small hotel. We reserved a room for five but somehow needed to get word of our revised location to both Sascha and Meredith, presumably still exploring Estrella. Knowing they would eventually head our way, we went back to the dirt path, just past the fountain, and scratched a message into the ground with a sharp stick. It was the kind of trick I would have employed when I was eight years old, like crafting a makeshift telephone by connecting two cans together with a piece of string, or signaling the kids across the street with a flashlight during a dark summer night.

Sure enough, it worked. When Meredith and Sascha saw our rudimentary S.O.S., they veered off the path and found their way to our hotel. They hopped into hot showers before easing themselves into the deep-cushioned recesses of the room's two armchairs. Jess had whipped up a feast of rice, spinach, and fish in our galley kitchen. Fed and bathed, we were happy as clams.

We were already a full day behind my original schedule, but no one seemed to mind. As the old saying goes, "Man plans, God laughs." Late that night I scribbled in my journal, "I feel the first spark of the Camino taking over me. I feel stronger. Perhaps my metamorphosis is beginning." Day three was in the books.

June Cleaver

"I once was lost, but now am found,
was blind, but now I see."

—John Newton, *Amazing grace!*

I was the one who carried the guidebook during our trip. It was the only text important enough to make the cut and end up in my backpack. During our time on the Camino, I filled its margins with notes and spent hours each evening staring at the maps in the back index. Even as a young girl, I was captivated by cartography, fascinated by how the whole world could be carved into manageable bites by longitude and latitude.

Family vacations, in particular, would be ripe with opportunities for me to chart our itinerary's course, memorizing the names of towns, lakes, rivers, and every highway attraction along the way. Navigation came easily to me. So easily, in fact, that after each trip I would retain close-to-flawless recall of every road and turn. Even years later, I could still find my way back to each location by "feel." I instinctively knew which way to turn when I arrived at a crossroad. Guided by an internal compass, I seemed to always know where I was.

I share this trait with my father. My mother, by contrast, couldn't find her way out of a paper bag.

One day I tried to teach her a surefire way to remember her left from her right, a skill I thought would help with her constant disorientation. I held out my left hand, pointing my index finger and thumb in a 90-degree angle. "Look Mom," I said encouragingly. "Your left hand makes a capital 'L.' That's how you can remember." She looked at me as if I were speaking a foreign language and wearily shook her head.

My sense of spatial awareness was innate; a handy talent that allowed me to continually recalibrate to true north, both literally and figuratively. I would grow to depend on it.

It is ironic, then, that my childhood hero was Amelia Earhart, the famed pilot who lost her way never to be found again. I first learned about her while in elementary school; she was the only woman to be included in a course of study dominated by dead white men. It was the 1960s, after all. Had it not been for Louisa May Alcott, Betsy Ross, and the witch trials of Salem, my entire grade school curriculum might have been devoid of double x chromosomes.

In Earhart, I discovered someone who bucked convention in a different sort of way. She was rakish in both attitude and appearance. She exuded a sassiness I dared not express. Lanky and boyish, she fought her way into the male-dominated world of aviation, becoming the first woman to fly solo across the Atlantic Ocean. She was not deterred by even the most daunting of challenges. As far as Amelia was concerned, the world was her oyster.

Hoping to circumnavigate the globe, Earhart was making good progress on what was to be her last flight when she headed toward Howland Island to refuel. But somehow, she fell off course. She lost radio contact and, without it, any hope of navigating to safety. In one of the most enduring mysteries of the 20th century,

Earhart's plane was never recovered, nor were her remains or those of her navigator Frederick Noonan. It is a disquieting thought to imagine her scanning the horizon of the Pacific, desperate for a glimpse of land during that long-ago July of 1937.

Decades later, in July of 1999, a similar fate would befall John F. Kennedy Jr. as the ocean and sky of the Atlantic became inverted, leading his Piper Saratoga to spiral into the sea. I was living in Falmouth that summer, a small town on Cape Cod just across the water from Martha's Vineyard, Kennedy's destination that doom-filled day. I remember hearing the whir of helicopters the morning after the crash as they hovered off the coast, looking for debris, or casualties, or both. Like Earhart, he would never again be seen alive.

Kennedy's death lingered in my heart, partly because of its similarity to the idol of my youth. But despite these unnerving stories, I never lost my own lust to explore. It was an heirloom passed on to me by my mother, an adventuresome spirit who spent much of her life caged by convention and responsibility. I can still see her in my mind's eye, stopping to gaze out over the churning ocean waves during those countless beach walks of my youth. The wind would be in her face. Her hair, blown straight back off her forehead. Her eyes would water behind the big, circular sunglasses housewives wore at the time, inspired by the fashion styles of Jackie Onassis. But it was the look on her face I remember most, a pain and longing deeply etched into her brow.

For the rest of my life, I would feel tension between us. She was so smart and so talented. But she was a ringleader without a ring. One moment she would push me to make the most of the changing landscape for women; the next she would resent me for doing so.

She had June Cleaver. I had Mary Tyler Moore. It was never a fair fight.

During her lighter moments, she would regale me with stories of her abbreviated career as a hospital chemist. It was a "glory days" kind of banter that included tales of cheeky co-workers and difficult diagnostic assessments. She worked tirelessly at Dr. Joslin's side, looking for chemical combinations to treat his growing number of diabetic patients. He took her opinions and her work seriously, a rare thing in those days.

Not surprisingly, my favorite story of my mother's was of a late night spent in her preferred spot, her beloved laboratory. She was pouring some sort of solution from one flask into another when a portion of it spilled, splashing onto the front of her scrubs.

Although she was wearing protective gloves, eyewear, and a lab coat, the solvent still splattered across much of her abdomen. Instinctively jumping back, she was relieved when nothing seemed awry. But then she felt a strange sensation, like a small tear had begun. Within a few seconds, the girdle she was wearing let loose. The cocktail she had mixed left her cotton pants unscathed but had dissolved her synthetic girdle upon impact. Such were the dangers of life as a chemist, she jauntily declared.

But those stories were few and far between. Soon after starting at the hospital, she met my father. She too was living in a boarding house, this one located at 25 Autumn Street, just around the corner from the hospital. It was an easy commute, particularly for those, like her, who worked the night shift. She would often head to a nearby diner for dinner prior to starting her shift. My Dad, weary from a long day at the office, stopped in to the same diner one night for an early supper. Over a blue plate special, their lives came together.

There would be no Earhart-esque exploits in my mother's future after that, in large part because she would need to corral her life within the confines dictated by my father's disability. To her credit, she saw past his physical limitations, choosing him instead for his strength of character. But it would prove to be a lonesome life. If she dreamt of adventures, she would have to do them alone. And that just wasn't done in those days.

When I decided to walk the Camino, my mother was already in her mid-80s. Her short-term memory had been compromised due to a number of small strokes, making her diabetes even more difficult to manage. Both of these conditions affected her health significantly.

I didn't tell her I was headed to Spain to traverse its 500-mile expanse. I knew she wouldn't remember. I also didn't have the emotional bandwidth to endure a withering critique or a barrage of churlish questions. But that didn't keep me from thinking of her during that 40-day stretch. In fact, she was never far from my thoughts. My mother was the reason behind so much of what drew me to the Camino in the first place. If not for her, I wouldn't have the fortitude to even make the attempt.

While I admire her bravery, I am no Amelia Earhart. And while I lament my mother's regrets, they are not my own. I imagine Earhart would have appreciated the physicality of the Camino, the grit it demanded, and the adventuresome spirit it required. I imagine my mother would have appreciated the dark emotional hue of the pilgrimage, how it stripped bare its protagonists, and how it lent itself to ruminations on faith, solitude, and purpose.

During my time on the trail, I began to understand the differences between being a traveler and being a pilgrim. The traveler enjoys moving through the world, seeing new things, and appreciating new experiences. But the pilgrim *searches* the world, listening for the voice that beckons, calling them deeper into their interior life.

Three days into the Camino, I was still a traveler. But that would change soon enough.

Neon Underwear

"Modesty is a vastly overrated virtue."

—John Kenneth Galbraith

As soon as I exited the hotel, I promptly fell off the curb. I winced as my left ankle turned, sending a shockwave of pain up my shin. On the rare occasion I do lose my balance, I can usually catch myself. But the added weight of the backpack threw me off kilter. I was on the ground before I knew it.

My ankle would be fine, but both of my knees absorbed a good whack at the end my tumble. It was not a good omen as the day's itinerary began with a steep climb up to Villamayor de Monjardin, elevation 2,132 feet (650 m), population 150. We nicknamed the hill "Madonna's Boob," due to its uncanny resemblance to the cone-shaped brassieres the singer had worn in her heyday. While we giggled at the thought, "Mount Madonna" got the last laugh. By the time I reached the crest of Monjardin, my thighs and lungs were on fire.

I discovered a surprising nook during the ascent, a large sunken bath framed by beautiful stone arches. Fuente de los Moros (Fountain of the Moors) was a 13th-century pool of deliciousness. Dark and private, it would have been the perfect spot to skinny dip, had the water been warmer.

Reluctantly, I continued past the bath and into a quaint church named San Andrés. After sitting on a hard wooden pew for some 15 minutes, I lit a candle and moved on. It's best not to stop for too long while hiking. Inertia begets inertia.

The rest of the afternoon's walk was pleasant and flat. I was bound on both sides by hip-high haulms of flaxen grain. It was a feast for the eyes. As I neared Los Arcos, I ran across a pilgrim who had set up his tent in someone's garden. He smoked quietly while poised atop a stone wall, content to just stare out at the scenery. He was the picture of serenity. An example to consider emulating, I mused.

After loping into town, I stopped at a small store, bought a Coca Cola, and drank it lustfully while propping my feet up on a nearby chair. Sascha, Jess, and Beth soon rolled through and all of us made our way to the albergue, a 70-bed dormitory named Isaac Santiago. Flashing our pilgrim passports at the front desk, we claimed a handful of bunk beds next to one another. Some in our group headed to the showers while the rest of us watched the packs. Then we reversed roles until everyone had removed the day's accumulation of dust and sweat.

As the trip progressed, we became much more savvy about how best to select our sleeping quarters for the night. First and foremost, we would hunt for bunks that were located far away from the entryway and showers. We would also try to distance ourselves from men, especially those with pot bellies who tended to sleep on their backs. Sweet though they may have been while awake, they often shook the rafters at night. Snoring until dawn. We did anything we could to separate ourselves from our burly compatriots, even if it meant going to bed before 8:00 p.m. in hopes of getting to sleep before the cacophony began.

We were still new to the game when we arrived in Los Arcos. We picked a string of lower bunks in the middle of the room. We wouldn't do that again.

Meredith and I chose adjacent lower bunks. After showering, we were sitting on our cots chatting when the man who had chosen the bunk above Meredith came strutting out of the bathroom. He had on a pair of exceedingly small blue neon underwear, speedo style. It didn't take long for him to join our conversation. Standing over us, he never made a move to put on his pants. Meredith, now trapped on the lower bunk, tried gracefully to continue the conversation with this man's bulge resting at her eye level, just a few inches away from the end of her nose. Still a teenager and having been raised in a strict Muslim home, she was mortified. Both by his cavalier behavior and his inability to read the room.

When we were finally able to extricate ourselves, we turned the corner to exit into the courtyard, only to intercept another man sauntering out of the shower area with his towel casually draped over his ... shoulder. Modesty, apparently, wasn't a high priority on the Camino.

At dinner, we met a quirky pilgrim from Vancouver named Evelyn. Like Chicago, she was an older woman and solo hiker. I would come to find out later on why she was doing the trek on her own. But that night we just drank Sangria and laughed.

Despite the blisters cropping up like mushrooms on her feet, Beth was beginning to feel more comfortable. We had covered just over 40 miles. We were finally hitting our stride.

Duct Tape

"People will forget what you said, people will forget what you did, but people will never forget how you made them feel."

—Maya Angelou

Duct tape was, by far, the most essential item in my backpack. If there were only one item I could recommend to every pilgrim, it would be duct tape. Prior to the Camino, I had never heard of this magical hiking elixir. While I would become a true disciple during the trip, Beth remained skeptical. Her conversion would come too late.

It was Jess who first divulged this hikers' secret to me. The proper protocol, as she explained it, was to carefully apply tape to each part of your foot prone to blistering. For some people, that was the back of the heel. For others, it was the big toe or perhaps the ball of the foot. Wherever your hot spots most often developed, that was the area to cover. Once you had wrapped each foot, you could pull on your sock and boot for the day without worry.

She insisted the duct tape be applied directly to the skin. No other band aids or moleskin were necessary. Just the tape. That sounded crazy to me. "What about when I need to take the tape *off?*" I asked dubiously. At the end of the day, when my feet were tender and sore, *that* was the time I was going to rip the duct tape off my bare skin?

"Don't worry," Jess assured me. "It will work."

On day five, awakened before 6:00 a.m. by the clatter of church bells, I dutifully taped my feet just after the sun rose. Our final destination for the day was Viana, just under 12 miles (18.6 km) away. Although the path was flat, the dirt was deeply rutted and difficult to traverse. Beth was struggling and stopped many times to adjust her pack and, at one point, removed both of her boots to check how her blisters were faring.

While she sat on the edge of the path, Evelyn strolled by and offered her some "second skin" band aids. Beth gratefully accepted, but they didn't make much of a difference. By that point, Jess was well ahead of us. Sascha and Meredith had also made easy work of the first few miles and were patiently waiting when Beth and I arrived at the village of Sansol. We were only 4+ miles (7 km) into the day, but Beth's feet were already too raw to continue.

As we headed up a short hill into town, Beth spotted a bus stop. She decided to take the bus for the last 7 or so miles (11.6 km), covering the remaining terrain in just 15 minutes. It turned out to be a prudent choice – the path descended precipitously just outside of Sansol and then rose steeply to the crest of Alto N.S. del Poyo, some 1,870 feet (570 m) high. I joined her, not wanting her to take the ride alone.

Once in Viana, we meandered into a café on the plaza of Santa Maria and waited for the rest of the team. Adjacent to the quadrangle was an albergue run by the Episcopal Church. We both agreed this was a great option for the night. This would be our chance to line up early and reserve bunks for the group.

We soon spotted Jess. She had made remarkable time. The three of us left the café and sat down on a bench in the sun. It had been a cold few days. Our bones needed a good warming. Soon another hiker joined us. "Dublin," as we nicknamed him, was on his second beer by that point, tipping the bottom of his glass skyward as the clock tower chimed 11:00 a.m. He seemed pleased to have found a new audience and we listened attentively as he told us about his life.

His wife had died four years earlier. Looking for a way to recalibrate, he had considered walking the Camino. He worked in Ireland leading hiking tours. He was fit. He had the gear. But he had four children still living at home; parenthood had put his dream on hold.

When Ireland's economy soured, he sensed the time was right. He started his journey in St. Jean Pied-de-Port, eager to traverse every mile the pilgrimage had to offer. During his first couple of days, he came across a backpack and a pair of sandals that had been left on the side of the road.

This, all of us would learn, was a common occurrence. Nearly every pilgrim brings too much and, straining under the weight, abandons items, even valuable ones, during moments of discomfort or fatigue. After determining the items had been left on purpose, Dublin swapped out his heavy boots for the sandals. In exchange, he left some sterling coins in a zippered side pocket. A week later he ran into an excited German pilgrim who told him he had found an abandoned rucksack with some money tucked in a small side cavity. Dublin just smiled and nodded.

When Sascha and Meredith rolled in, we laid down on the warm stones of the plaza to wait for the albergue to open. We watched a handful of kids kick a soccer ball around while dogs drank from the town's fountain. But mostly we slept, right there on the ground, placing our heads together and fanning out like a grubby starfish.

I woke the group from our collective nap when the front door of the hostel opened. We dutifully listened to the rules and were then assigned a room of our own, big enough to accommodate all five of us. But privacy had a price. There were only mats on the floor of our designated area, no beds. The temperature was so cold that night I kept my hat on for the duration and wore Beth's spare pair of wool socks over my hands. Between the nippy air and the hard, wooden floor, sleep was evasive.

Because it was a religious facility, we were asked to attend that evening's worship service. This included a chat with the local parish priest about our motivations for walking the Camino. We were joined by a man from Spain's Basque region, a Swiss woman, a young German, a man from Slovakia with a particularly bad combover, and a gentleman from Holland who had biked all the way from his home before even starting the pilgrimage.

After Mass, we were roped into preparing dinner by our hosts before sitting down as a group to eat. We were a motley crew. Without regular access to a laundromat, we had turned a bit rank. This unfortunate commonality was made easier to stomach after a generous dose of peppermint mist was sprayed on all of us by a Reiki practitioner living at the albergue.

The following morning, we learned the bicycle belonging to the Dutchman had been stolen during the night. As we set out, he was lamenting his fate to the Viana police department. That was the last we saw of him.

It was Fathers' Day, at least in the States, and my heart was heavy. I had hoped the Camino would give me a chance to move my grieving process along. My father's death still seemed so raw, like a scab that never quite managed to heal. The holiday was just another reminder I was still struggling with the loss.

Beth, on the other hand, was occupied by a much more pedestrian problem. As she slogged along beside me, she was beleaguered by a new set of blisters. We walked haltingly to Logroño, a university town where the flavor of the medieval and the modern makes for an interesting blend. Just a hair under 6 miles (9.5 km), the path we had traversed was blessedly flat. The vineyards of the La Rioja region began to disappear behind us, replaced by the bars and nightlife typical of a college locale.

While Sascha, Meredith, and Jess continued to Navarette, Beth elected to ride the bus for the second consecutive day. It was hard to imagine another option. The condition of her feet, combined with the challenge ahead – close to 8 additional miles (12.4 km) including a rise in elevation of over 100 meters – made this a reasonable choice. Still, I chafed at the thought. I found the constant starting and stopping to be frustrating. It annoyed me that I hadn't yet gained a sense of rhythm or momentum. I was also concerned this string of shortened days would cause me to lose the level of fitness I had worked so hard to achieve. Torn between being selfish and feeling bitter, I opted for bitter. But I knew I needed to find a new mindset and fast. If the Camino was truly a journey and not simply a destination, as I had often touted prior to our coming to Spain, I needed to walk the walk and not just talk the talk.

We were joined on the bus by a huge gaggle of hikers headed to various spots on the trail. We hopped out at Navarette and bid the remaining riders goodbye, knowing we would not be able to walk fast enough to cross their paths again. Our hostel that night was a bit upscale, offering us five beds and access to a handful of washing machines, all for just 50 Euros. Once in our room, we gleefully began to peel off our clothes until we realized we had just one spare outfit.

Whatever we kept on would miss a much-needed spin in the wash. Beth, the only parent among us, devised the solution. We would strip down to our "all togethers," as Sascha called it, wearing only our rain ponchos cinched by a belt. This made our already short ponchos that much shorter, but it meant *everything* could go into the wash. For the duration of the cycle, we each walked and sat down carefully, so as not to flash anyone unnecessarily.

Afterwards, we hung everything out to dry on the balcony railing, with the exception of Jess' multi-colored thongs. Those were placed tactfully on the radiator in our room. As we laughed and talked on the veranda, clothed scantily in only our ponchos, I felt my shoulders relax. It had been a good day, even if it hadn't gone exactly as planned. Perhaps that was the message my father was sending me on this special day, so discreet I almost missed it.

Take a breath. Look around you. Enjoy the moment.
If you don't let go, you'll never be able to move on.

I fell asleep that night as soon as my head hit the pillow. The Camino was wearing me down, in the very best kind of way. Tomorrow, the longest day of the year, was filled with promise. I vowed I would "turn the page," so to speak, and approach the dawn of the next day with an entirely new attitude.

How was I to know what awaited me would do precisely the opposite? Pulling me back into the same morass I had spent my whole life trying to escape.

Epiphany

n. An appearance or revelation.
The perception of the essential nature or
meaning of something.

Stuck in Reverse

"An adult human consists of sedimentary layers.
We shed more skins than we can count, and are born
each day to a merciful forgetfulness. We forget most of our
past but embody all of it."

—John Updike, *Rabbit Run*

They say when someone finally makes the decision to take their own life, a strange calm comes over them. All of the tumult and angst about what to do, about how to survive another day, is put to rest. They know the pain will end. They are, at last, in control.

The same was true of CeCe, although most of us didn't recognize the clues. Taking her upbeat tone at face value, we thought she was getting better.

Which is partly why it staggered me to read of her death that day in Azofra, a jarring bolt bathed in the comforting indigo glow of the computer screen. I had only been away for a week at that point. How had so much changed in such a small amount of time?

Unlike me, CeCe's two closest friends were not so easily duped. After a quick trip to California to visit her family, to say goodbye to them as it turned out, CeCe left a note for her housemate after returning home. The message affixed to the refrigerator said she had decided to take an extra night away. Betsy and Julie came across the stray wisp of paper later that day. The note was simple and direct, perfunctory even. But instinctually they knew something was wrong. Terribly wrong.

They contacted the police and relayed their suspicions. In hopes of discerning her whereabouts, the authorities tracked her credit card activity. It took some time but eventually they discovered a charge had made to a local hotel. Betsy and Julie made their way there. As they waited at the far end of a hallway, the fire department broke the door down. Their fears were confirmed. The police verified CeCe was indeed inside. Present but long gone.

In retrospect, the signs seemed frighteningly clear: the euphoria; the circuit of goodbyes; even the smallest of details methodically finalized prior to her death. CeCe had been meticulous in her planning, including a last-minute cancellation of her cable service and a transfer of money into her checking account sufficient to cover the burial costs. She had spent her final hours writing letters to those she loved. She had thought it all through.

The presence of this kind of intentionality unnerved me; it was far easier to believe CeCe's death by suicide occurred during a moment of intense grief and pain. A spontaneous combustion of sorts, where the coincidence of opportunity and means made for a tragic end. But to know she had painstakingly arranged every piece of the puzzle prior to the act was heartbreakingly revealing.

This is why those who are left behind are so often haunted by the "what ifs." What if I had spent more time with her? What if I had listened more attentively? What if I called more frequently, or insisted she continue with therapy, or refused to keep the secrets she had shared in confidence?

What if, what if, what if.

After reading the news of CeCe's death, my longest day on the Camino turned into my longest night. During fitful clusters of dozing, I dreamt I was trying to sleep on the side of a steep hill. Tangled in my sleeping bag, I struggled to hold on to the crumbling dirt beneath me, desperate to keep from rolling off the incline into a deep abyss. I woke up with a start, sweating and exhausted.

I imagined all of my Harvard colleagues huddled together back in Cambridge, holding each other up as best they could. I was heartsick. I was in shock. And I was feeling very removed from where I felt I needed to be.

Amidst the undulating hills of rural Spain, my interior landscape was wildly out of step with my exterior one. I was torn about where my responsibilities now lay. Neither choice – staying in Spain or leaving for home – would alleviate me of my guilt or assuage my regret.

In the end, I made the decision to continue with the pilgrimage rather than return to the States. Before setting out the next morning, I went back to the church where Jess and I had drawn our original note, "Jess and Anne were here. Gone to the bar to eat." Underneath the text I added the postscript, "RIP CeCe." This was where I would say goodbye.

Of course, it wouldn't be that easy. Like an onion that had been peeled, CeCe's death revealed a tender layer of skin I had fought hard to conceal.

The Camino was about moving forward. But suddenly, I was stuck in reverse.

The Perils of Peanut Butter

"When you repress or suppress those things which
you don't want to live with, you don't really solve
the problem, because you don't bury the problem
dead – you bury the problem alive.
It remains alive and active inside you."

—Father John Powell

We had made our way across 10 miles (15.2 km) of hills and
fertile farmland before reaching Santo Domingo de la Calzada.
Our efforts were well rewarded. As we rambled up the town's
main street, we discovered what turned out to be the nicest
place we had found thus far. Casa del Santo had 83 beds, leather
couches, spotless bathrooms, and wrought-iron stairwells. Most
importantly, it was situated smack in the middle of the Old
Quarter. Convenient and low cost, it was just what the doctor
ordered.

We left our packs with the person at the front desk and went
to find lunch. I was over the moon when we stumbled upon a
traditional Italian restaurant. I gleefully ordered a heaping plate
of spaghetti Bolognese and I enjoyed every bite. It was the first
real comfort food I had found during the trip.

Having eaten more than enough, we pushed our chairs away from the table and headed back to the albergue, stopping at a small market to buy ingredients for that night's salad. Loaded with supplies, we were good to go.

But in the process of restocking our packs, we realized a good deal of food had gone missing. Maybe we had lost track after more than a week of walking? Perhaps we had left items at our last hostel? While possible, both explanations seemed unlikely. We were stumped.

The more I thought about it, the stranger it seemed. The mystery was solved soon after. Later that day, Jess discovered Sascha sitting in the hostel eating peanut butter straight out of the jar. He had removed it in secret, hoping to eat his fill before anyone realized it was gone.

She was upset, as were Meredith and I. While the three of us left to attend an evening vespers service, a commitment we had made earlier with a handful of Cistercian nuns, Beth remained at the albergue to have a heart-to-heart with Sascha.

Despite her gentle reproach and quite unexpectedly, he began to cry. He was ashamed of his actions and told Beth he had long struggled with his relationship to food, concealing his binging for years.

It had been easy to manufacture such moments on the Camino. Sascha had regularly eaten more than his fair share, consistently isolating himself on numerous occasions so he could eat without detection. Unwittingly, we had helped by asking him to carry food for the entire group. Not surprisingly, this temptation proved too hard to resist.

When I returned to the hostel, I went upstairs to check on him. He apologized profusely, much more upset at the thought he had disappointed me than about draining our stash. Painful though it was, Jess' discovery allowed us to clear the air. Sascha's honesty brought the group back together or, more precisely, brought him back into the group. Once again, we were all on the same page.

What I didn't know, until years later, was that the infamous "peanut butter incident" was tied to another complicating set of circumstances. Unbeknownst to me, as Sascha was nearing the end of his time at Andover, he began taking an anti-anxiety medication. It worked like a charm, allowing him to finish his high school career healthier in both mind and spirit. With the stress of grades, graduation, and admission into college now behind him, he decided the time was right to stop taking his prescription. So just prior to leaving for Spain, Sascha quit cold turkey. This was in direct contradiction to the recommended practice that called for a slow and supervised weaning from his medication. The consequences of his more abrupt approach were swift and substantial.

During our first week together, I noticed a change in Sascha. He seemed off somehow, fragile and detached in a way I couldn't quite put my finger on. In actuality, his body was in the throes of withdrawal. But all I saw were behaviors that made me question whether the two of us were going to be able to cooperatively complete the pilgrimage as planned.

But as the trip progressed, Sascha's body began to recover and recalibrate. His compulsive eating subsided and his emotional equilibrium returned. Soon enough, he was back to his old self, easing any concerns I had about the long-term viability of our partnership.

What wasn't as easy to confront was how this kerfuffle triggered some of my own issues with food. As is often the case, Sascha's errant behavior allowed me to conveniently dismiss my own role in what had happened. Despite all of my pre-walk preparation, a gnawing insecurity still lingered. What if I wasn't strong enough to finish? What if the pilgrimage proved me to be an imposter, someone whose big plans were replaced with even bigger excuses?

If I failed, not only would I know, but *everyone* would know. And failure, as I had learned long ago, was not an option.

So, I did what I always did. I planned for every possible scenario. But this time, I had enlisted Sascha to help control my fears. If he shouldered the supply of food, I would be spared the worry of having enough water or nourishment to sustain me during those long and taxing days. The idea of being stranded in the rural isolation of the Camino, without proper rations, scared me. But instead of approaching the pilgrimage as an opportunity to more fully embrace uncertainty, I had taken the easy way out, pretending chivalry gone awry, and not apprehension, had placed Sascha at the center of the maelstrom. He would be the protective shield behind which I could hide my own food-related issues. He would do the emotional dirty work for me.

While the peanut butter provided Sascha with succor, it provided me with security. I *needed* that peanut butter, good old-fashioned Skippy peanut butter. But not in the run-of-the-mill kind of way. It was much more convoluted than that.

For as far back as I can remember, I have tried to manage a very tender digestive system. Back before "gluten-free" and "lactose intolerant" were part of the larger cultural lexicon, there were no words to explain my daily dose of abdominal misery. I was raised in the "clean your plate" era, where pushing aside unwanted food was tantamount to starving fellow children on continents unknown.

Defying my dinner plate, which was in essence to defy my mother, was out of the question. Which left me with only one option. Night after night I ate what was put in front of me, followed by a tall glass of cold milk. Within 15 minutes I would feel horrible, stomach churning and abdomen cramping. It was painful and debilitating and, as I grew older, embarrassing. Always needing a bathroom close by was a necessity that only grew exponentially more challenging. The stress of childhood sleepovers and camping trips was soon replaced by concerns related to commuting, carpooling, air travel, or any situation where a restroom was not immediately accessible.

On the eve of my twelfth birthday, my mother asked me what I might like as a gift.

With eyes rooted to the kitchen floor I answered, "I don't want to drink milk anymore."

"Don't be silly," she parried. "What do you *really* want?"

"Really Mom, please don't make me drink any more milk."

It had never occurred to anyone how odd it was that I was the only kid in the neighborhood who didn't eat ice cream, or who never wanted whipped cream on pancakes, or who nervously munched on toast hoping no one would notice the plateful of scrambled eggs surreptitiously hidden under my napkin. While my mother eventually acquiesced to my odd request, milk was the only item that disappeared from the menu. The others continued to be served on a regular basis.

Eating became an activity so fraught with anxiety that I narrowed what I was willing to consume to just a handful of things. After college, my friends and co-workers would playfully joke about my juvenile eating habits. My rudimentary diet was routinely fodder for conversational jabs. Eating at fancy restaurants, trying exotic foods, developing a taste for fine wines, all seemed part and parcel of what it meant to be an adult.

But not for me. Over time, I developed a strategy for every occasion. I would eat before going to parties or get-togethers if I was uncertain what would be served. Demurely declining food at meetings or social events was never questioned, at least not if you were a woman. People just assumed you were dieting. With friends it was harder. What they viewed as teasing, I viewed as hurtful. More often than not I would smile and nod, but underneath I was bruised by their running commentary. In response, I tried everything I could to keep my eating habits off the radar.

I was aware of this foible, even when I was alone. Whenever I left the house, I tucked a few granola bars in my pocket, even if I was just running a quick errand. Every bag I carried had lifesavers, gum, raisins, or peanuts lodged into a zippered pocket, "just in case." Beth would often comment on the girth of my "feed bag" when we went on trips, nearly as heavy as my actual carry-on luggage. It wasn't that I regularly ate from the supply. I just needed to have it nearby; it was an emotional crutch on which I had come to depend.

It came as no surprise then, at least to me, that I reacted with anger after discovering the peanut butter stash had dwindled precipitously. But the person I should have been mad at wasn't Sascha.

It was me.

The wisdom of the Camino encourages its travelers to unburden themselves, particularly of their fears. Each backpack provided a window into the trepidations of its owner, stuffed to the gills with presumed antidotes for every uncertainty.

The trick for me wasn't to find a bigger backpack, but to find comfort in my own discomfort. What was it going to take, I wondered, for me to *really* let go?

The Beginning of the End

"We want to do a lot of stuff; we're not in great shape.
We didn't get a good night's sleep.
We're a little depressed. Coffee solves all these problems
in one delightful little cup."

—Jerry Seinfeld

When we left the next morning, each of us had decided on a different course of action. We concurred Viloria de la Rioja would be our final destination for the day, just over 8 miles (13.2 km) from our starting point in Santo Domingo. Most of the day would be spent ascending a gradual incline, a rise of close to 650 feet (200 m), that included a steep dip and steeper upslope. We crossed our fingers that shortening the overall distance for the day would make that V-slant a bit more palatable. At least that was the theory.

Meredith, Jess, and I headed out just after daybreak, leaving Sascha and Beth to snooze. They had decided to take the bus that day, and so had plenty of time for a leisurely breakfast.

After a bit of food, they packed their things and headed to the town's bus stop. When the driver arrived, Sascha attempted, using some basic Spanish and a collection of hand signals, to purchase two tickets to Viloria. But there was no bus to Viloria. They had misread the schedule. With no other option available, they were forced to exit at Redecilla del Camino and then walk the remaining 2.5 miles (4 km), including the very dip they had been hoping to avoid.

Jess arrived to our destination first, well ahead of the group. It was a virtual ghost town. No services, stores, or restaurants were to be found. She wasn't tired but her stomach was growling. She had set off for the day, as she often did, without eating breakfast. Now in a pickle, she chastised herself for not stopping at the small coffee shop she had seen back in Redecilla. As she was mulling over her options, Sascha and Beth strolled into town. Jess, sensing an opportunity, convinced Beth a cup of coffee was worth backtracking. Reversing course, they did just that.

Up the hill twice. Down the hill twice. All for two cups of coffee.

Meredith and I, moving more slowly, meandered into Redecilla and walked right by the café, choosing instead to buy our wares at a small mom-and-pops store on the far side of the town square. After a brief snack, we headed toward Viloria, only to be passed by our then hyper-caffeinated teammates. They wore those additional 5 miles like a badge of honor. But all that java eventually wore off.

While stopped at the top of a particularly steep hill, I could see Beth turn around to face me. She was at the crest of one peak. I was at the crest of the other. A lush valley of grass lay between us.

We were now stationed at both summits, perhaps a half mile or so apart, and the interceding ravine made for wonderful acoustics. She cupped her hands around her mouth and I heard her bellow, "We could have just gone to Weight Watchers!" I wasn't quite sure if she was joking or mad as hell. I hoped it was the former.

Once all of us had reached Viloria, it was clear we would need to continue. For reasons unknown, the albergue there was not open. Without food or shelter, there was no choice but to keep walking.

We set our sights next on Villamajor del Río, just over 2 miles (3.4 km) down the road. Luckily the hostel there was open year-round, offering 52 beds spread across nine rooms. The proprietor gave us a room of our own. After settling in, we headed to the only restaurant in town. It was not exactly what we were expecting.

As we ducked inside, we were met by two enormous pig legs, flesh roasted and dangling from the ceiling by the hoof. Meredith instinctually recoiled. I too was taken aback, not because I didn't eat pork, but because I found the traditional Spanish cuisine not to be compatible with strenuous exercise. I craved a ripe apple, an icy glass of water, or a plateful of chicken and vegetables. Instead, the menu was heavy with pork entrees, stews, and full-bodied red wines.

Walking such long distances had actually diminished my appetite. Like Meredith, I scanned the menu for anything other than pork or alcohol.

After eating our fill, we spent the rest of the afternoon relaxing in the yard behind the albergue, swapping stories and watching laundry flap on the clothesline of a distant farmhouse. The picturesque environs made for a lovely respite. But there was something else, a disquieting feeling in the midst of this bucolic scene. A ribbon of melancholy ran just underneath our chatter.

Just 34 miles (55.2 km) to the west was Burgos, the terminus for Jess, Meredith, and Beth. Each had jobs and other commitments that required they return home. While their early exit had always been the plan, their imminent departure made me sad and feeling a bit unsettled. Sascha and I would traverse the rest of the Camino on our own. For the rest of the "Fab Five," the beginning of the end was near.

The author, Beth, Sascha, and Meredith (from left to right)

A Heart's Desire

"You must do the thing you think you cannot do."

—Eleanor Roosevelt

After literally walking in reverse the day before, Jess came to me with an entirely different plan in mind when the sun rose in Villamajor. Our pace, as a group, was considerably slower than I had initially imagined, positing us well behind our original schedule. Jess was the only one who had walked every mile of the pilgrimage. She was determined to complete the remaining distance, but given her flight was in just three short days, she knew she needed to make it to Burgos in two. I could see it was important to her to achieve the goal she had set for herself. She would need to strike out on her own if she had any hope of doing so.

Reluctantly, I agreed to her proposal. We arranged to meet at the Catedral de Santa Maria, a 13th-century gothic church in the center of Burgos' main plaza, two days hence. Before the trip began, Beth had made a reservation at Mesón del Cid, a beautiful hotel located just across from the cathedral. She thought we would need a treat by that point and I had concurred. Having our last night together in Spain in such luxurious surroundings sounded heavenly.

I knew there was a large fountain adjacent to the cathedral. We set it as our rendezvous point, knowing finding Jess amidst the throbbing crowds of the expansive plaza might otherwise feel like looking for a needle in a haystack.

This plan hinged on Jess' ability to traverse all 34 miles (55.2 km) in just two days. This journey would include scaling four peaks (Mojapán, Pedraja, Carnero, and Cruceiro), the tallest of which topped out at 3,444 feet (1,050 meters). The change in altitude (1,345 feet or 410 meters) would be challenging enough. Doing the mileage *and* the climb, particularly without the support of the group, was a tall order.

It also felt like something else might be at play. Jess, like every pilgrim, had come to the Camino in search of something. For her, the potential answer to her riddle had just four letters.

J-A-C-K. That was the name of the man she had started dating a few months prior to joining our ragtag pilgrimage posse. It had been a whirlwind romance, something that made her heart race with excitement. But there was trepidation as well.

Raised in a traditional family in a small rural town in New Hampshire, Jess grew up within the strictures of a rigid and conservative Christianity. She had held tight to this worldview throughout most of her life, including enrolling in a Christian college whose mission statement touted its "evangelical identity." By the time I met Jess, she had long since graduated and had moved to Los Angeles to work as a fashion designer. Returning to Boston's North Shore a few years later, she once again fell into step with many friends from her undergraduate years, including her then on-again, off-again boyfriend.

Beautiful, fit, funny, and charismatic, Jess turned heads on a regular basis. But many of her suitors fell away when they discovered she was serious about her faith. She didn't do the bar scene. She didn't sleep around. For most men in their twenties, her lifestyle was unfathomable.

I didn't know any of this when I met Jess during the first day of my new job. Truth be told, I wouldn't have guessed it either. She didn't look or act the part of a tightly wrapped Christian. Despite our 20-year age difference, there was an instant chemistry between us. I was convinced, right from the start, she would be my friend.

On Monday morning, the start of my second week at the job, Jess poked her head into my office.

"Hey!" she exclaimed, flashing a quick grin. "I just came to check on you. Do you mind if I sit down?"

"Of course not, come on in," I replied. "How was your weekend? What did you do?"

"It was my birthday on Saturday!" she gushed. "I had a great time. How about you?"

The question hovered between us, the silence growing increasingly awkward while I decided what to do. I certainly wasn't planning on having this conversation with my co-workers, at least not in the second week of my employment.

Carefully and deliberately, I answered, "I got married. To a ... woman."

"Shut UP!" she screamed, jumping up and closing the door behind her. All smiles, she dropped back into her chair. "Tell me EVERYTHING!"

Yup, Jess was going to be my friend.

At that juncture, she was seeing the man she had met and dated in college. On the outside, they seemed like a perfect match. They were both athletic, outdoorsy, shared many friends in common and, most importantly, held the same Christian beliefs. But when I saw them together, there was no magic. Jess seemed convinced the potency would emerge once they were intimate, but I remained unconvinced. There was a reason this relationship had stalled.

Eventually he broke it off, sending Jess into a tailspin. But then Jack came along.

Like so many others, the match was the result of an internet dating app. He wasn't an obvious choice at first blush, but their connection was undeniable. He was a Midwesterner who had found his way to Princeton and then to a job in Washington, D.C. Having been given the chance to study with the financial support of his employer, he had moved to Boston, enrolling as a graduate student in an international relations program.

But with his degree nearly in hand, he would be heading back to D.C., sooner than later. Further complicating things, his Ivy League pedigree intimidated Jess. She was afraid he would tire of her when their relationship relied more on their intellectual connection than their physical one.

There was one more thing, more problematic than all the rest. Jess wanted to be a mother. She was convinced this was her true vocation, right down in the marrow of her bones. But at 29, her window of opportunity was frighteningly slim. Her own mother had gone into menopause in her early thirties, and Jess had been told by her physician this was likely her fate as well.

How did she really feel about Jack? Was it possible to tease apart her desire for children from assessing her interest in this potential marriage? What would she do if it was already too late? Would Jack still want her if she couldn't have children? All of these thoughts, and no doubt many more, swirled in Jess' head. Two days alone on the Camino might be just what she needed to sort through the pile.

She wanted answers. She *needed* answers. Hopefully a grueling climb, isolated from everything but her own thoughts, would clear her mind enough to see them.

The Last Stand

"This is a song for you, far away, so far away.
This is a song for you, far away from me......"

—James Taylor, *Song For You Far Away*

In the wee hours of the morning, Jess darted down the red dirt path, eager to get an early start. The rest of us waved goodbye. Even though she was the one on her own now, I suddenly felt lonesome. As my mother used to say, "better to leave than to be left behind." How right she was.

It was also Beth's birthday. Just as Jess disappeared from sight, Sascha and Meredith turned towards her and burst into a rousing rendition of "Happy Birthday," complete with two-part harmony. She grinned as we huddled together for a quick group hug. Time for us to head out as well.

The plaza of Belorado, a town tucked into the canyon of Río Tirón, was 3.4 miles (5.5 km) from where we stood. In order to arrive in Burgos alongside Jess, at some point we would need to take a bus. After doing a bit of research, Belorado seemed like the best place to snag a ride. The walk that morning was straight up, a climb that rose to 2,657 feet (810 m) at its apex. Short and sweet turned into short and steep.

After arriving, we found our way to the bus stop and in 35 minutes covered the same terrain Jess would do by foot over the course of the next two days. As I gazed out the window, I wasn't as disappointed as I thought I'd be. After a short ride through the mountains, the road into Burgos cut through the vast industrial sprawl that ringed the city. The Camino had quickly devolved into a concrete wasteland, filled with warehouses and wire fencing. Missing this section didn't seem all that bad.

The bus dropped us within a stone's throw of the city center. Within a few minutes we were craning our necks at the cathedral's spires. The plaza was a beehive of activity, filled with stylishly dressed Spaniards, weary backpackers, and teenagers smoking cigarettes while draped across nearby benches and each other. Our hotel for the night, the stunning Mesón del Cid, stood at the top left-hand corner of the expanse. Check-in was still a few hours away, so Beth shopped while Meredith, Sascha, and I went to tour the cathedral.

At mid-afternoon, we made our way back to the hotel. We tossed our bags on the floor of the room and hit the showers. Sascha generously offered to do laundry for the entire group. He gathered up every scrap of clothing we had and set out for the laundromat, leaving Meredith, Beth, and me with nothing but towels for coverage. Scrubbed and clean, we slipped under the cool crisp sheets of the room's two double beds. Thoughts of spin and fluff cycles danced in our heads.

Sascha returned with our clean clothes in tow and we all got dressed for dinner. We ambled to the river's edge, pausing every now and then to window shop. Somehow Meredith snuck away and bought two small candles and a sparkler. At the end of our meal, our waitress stuck all three into a slab of chocolate cake and presented the fiery plate to Beth. All of the patrons dining at the restaurant that night joined in and sang a spirited version of "¡Feliz Cumpleaños!" It was quite a spectacle.

Now woozy from our sugar-induced haze, we left our table to join the crush of people strolling the Promenade. It was a wonderful evening. Eventually we circled back to the plaza, its cobblestones shimmering under the lanterns' steady glow. Beth and I broke left, toward the Mesón. Sascha and Meredith broke right, toward the municipal albergue. For the first time since we had landed in Pamplona, Beth and I were alone. Just one more day together and she would head home.

We decided during dinner to take shifts sitting at the fountain the next day. We wanted to be absolutely certain one of us would be there when Jess arrived. We spiced up our "guard duty" by placing bets on what time she would appear. Meredith won by a long shot when Jess lumbered in at 11:30 a.m., just 30 minutes past Meredith's prediction. Beth was stationed at the fountain when she came into sight. She was so exhausted she didn't speak, collapsing into Beth's arms for a much-needed hug.

A shower and some food revived her and we spent the remaining portion of the afternoon finding Jess a hotel. After completing every mile of the pilgrimage, she wanted to splurge her last night. With accommodations at an upscale hotel secured, we all headed to our respective lodgings for a nap, agreeing to meet at the fountain at 6:30 p.m. for our final night together in Spain.

As we fanned out, we ran into three of our favorite partners in crime – Dublin, Eileen (a woman from Ireland we had met a few days prior), and Evelyn. We chatted a bit before Dublin and Eileen went on their way. But Evelyn lingered.

When she initially had decided to walk the Camino, neither her husband or sons, all adults by that time, had shown any interest. She seemed relieved by this response, interpreting it as tacit approval of her doing this adventure on her own. But after almost two weeks on the trail, she had not heard from any of them, even by email. Their silence upset her and she now seemed ambivalent about returning home once her pilgrimage was complete. She revealed to us she had come to Spain, in part, to discern whether or not a significant transition was in order. As the answer came more clearly into focus, I'm not sure she liked it.

She looked free but very, very sad.

In response, Beth, Meredith, and Jess roped her into having an ice cream in hopes of lifting her spirits. Then all of us left to catch a few winks before dinner.

As luck would have it, Sascha's uncle was also in Burgos on vacation. Sascha asked if we minded if he parted ways and joined his uncle for supper. A fresh face was always welcome and off they went. The rest of us proceeded to the plaza to attend that evening's festival. As dusk drew near, hundreds of people came out of the woodwork and swarmed the streets. There were face-painting stalls, balloon venders, bands, and giant papier-mâché puppet heads balanced atop tall wooden sticks. Some were decorated as knights, some as kings; we even saw renditions of Fu Manchu and the Blues Brothers. But the most ubiquitous sighting that night were all the televisions, each one tuned to the same channel – the broadcast of the Spain v. Chile World Cup match. Every storefront, every bar, everywhere I looked I saw clusters of diehard fans huddled around a screen. Twice while we were trying to squeeze into a bar, the streets erupted with a long and pulsating shriek.

GOOOOOOOOOOOOOOOOOOOOOOOOOOOOOAL!

It looked like a lock for the Spaniards. Thank goodness.

When it got to be 9:00 p.m., Beth and I threw in the towel. Meredith and Jess would need to continue their search for a nightclub without us. I was tired and already beginning to feel a bit blue. The next morning Sascha and I were due to depart early, leaving Meredith, Jess, and Beth behind. As a trio, they would make their way to Madrid and on to their respective flights.

Their pilgrimage was now over.

Meredith was planning on coming to our hotel, along with Sascha, at the crack of dawn the next morning. But Jess was planning to sleep in, a luxurious diversion from our usual routine. The time had come to say goodbye.

I pulled her aside in the narrow alleyway on which we found ourselves, hoping to have a private moment. The others, sensing my motivation, drifted further down the street, stopping when they were safely out of earshot.

But there were no words. I couldn't possibly express how grateful I was that she had come on this journey with me, bringing her own zany brand of fun and playfulness to an often-grueling undertaking. Jess was the frosting of our fivesome, the sweet dollop everyone looked forward to at the end of a long day.

I hugged her close and whispered in her ear, "I love you." What else was there to say?

Beth and I returned to the hotel, stopping in the lobby to send a few brief emails before heading to our room. A sense of melancholy hovered between us. The impending separation would be difficult. We went to bed reluctantly, knowing sleep would only hasten the morning's arrival. But Spain wasn't quite done with us. Just after midnight, the sky burst into color. Fireworks rained down on the cathedral, lighting up the entire plaza in the process. We jumped out of bed and hopped over to the window. It was electrifying to see the gothic stone illuminated by such a vibrant spray of light. Mobs of people were dancing beneath us chanting, *"¡Viva España!"* Chile, we surmised, must have lost the match.

The fireworks continued for another 15 minutes or so, but the dancing and drinking were just getting started. As was I.

And Then There Were Two

> "Sometimes surrender means giving up trying to understand
> and becoming comfortable with not knowing."
>
> —Eckhart Tolle

When I opened my eyes the next morning, my first thought was of CeCe. Her memorial service had been held earlier that day, while I was still fast asleep on a different continent. The leaflets had been printed and the speakers had spoken and the casseroles had been served. Somewhere during the night, CeCe had officially become part of my past.

Meredith and Sascha were due to arrive at 6:30 a.m., so I swung my legs over the edge of the bed and began my morning ritual, covering every inch of my skin with sunblock. Then, without warning, I started to cry. Big, heavy tears dropped from my eyelashes onto the front of my t-shirt. My Coppertone glazing came to an abrupt stop.

I was wrenched back into the present by the sound of a knock on the door. Beth stood, crossed the room, and turned the knob. Meredith and Sascha filed in, right on time.

Seeing my tear-streaked cheeks, Meredith wordlessly sat down next to me. Her silent presence provided a surprising amount of comfort. In the meantime, Sascha did some last-minute packing and then they both headed down the stairs to wait. Alone again, Beth and I kissed and hugged and squeezed and cried. Now more than ever, I was glad she would be with Jess and Meredith for the final leg of her journey.

Meredith would be my last goodbye. I saw her standing at the bottom of the hotel stairway as I descended, like a sentry at her post. She was always exactly where I needed her to be, right up to the very end. I was so lucky she had joined our crew. More than she knew. More than I could say.

I pulled her in close without bothering to take off my backpack, a spontaneous and heartfelt tangle of interlocking arms. "Take care of my girl," I whispered to her. She smiled ever so slightly and nodded her assent. If I was the rudder of this ship, Meredith was the keel. I would miss her terribly.

Sascha's uncle, Jon, had come to see us off. As the three of us made our way across the plaza, I heard Beth yell from the window of our room, *"¡Buen Camino!"* I blew her a kiss and turned the corner, heading west toward the Meseta.

The plan for the day was to walk to Hornillos del Camino, a route that was exceedingly flat with the exception of a sharp incline leading to the top of Alto Meseta, hovering some 3,116 feet (950 m) high. This was followed by a dangerous descent aptly named Cuesta de Matamulos, or the "mule killer." Our work was cut out for us.

Jon accompanied us for a few miles, chatting breezily about this and that. As the three of us bumped along, I began to regain my composure. The casual banter proved to be a good distraction, allowing me to get my bearings, emotional and otherwise.

The Meseta, according to both legend and my guidebook, would prove a test of some significance. The middle fold of this tripartite journey was in sharp contrast with the portion we had just traversed. The landscape from St. Jean Pied-de-Port to Burgos was known for a rigorous start, but then gave way to the patchwork of vineyards for which the Rioja wine country was known. Pilgrims needn't fret too much about the availability of supplies along this stretch. This first section contained a good number of reasonably sized towns, separated by beautiful fields of wheat, poppies, and grapevines.

Conversely, the Meseta, a name based on the Spanish word for table (mesa), was a flat and arid plateau known for its blistering heat and monotonous visage. But in order to experience its frying pan sizzle, you first had to claw your way up. Once on top of the butte, the altitude and heat thwarted the growth of almost all vegetation. Shade from the sun was nearly non-existent. It was a windswept dustbowl, making the Meseta a tough road to hoe.

Our prescribed route for the day would cover 12.4 miles (20 km), including the climb. I wouldn't have much time to wallow given the difficulty of the terrain. Good news for my heart. Bad news for my legs.

Then, rather unexpectedly, the sidewalk disappeared. A gravel lane replaced the pavement, stretching out toward the horizon. The looming plank of the Meseta was finally in view. Time for Sascha's last goodbye.

He and Jon exchanged a quick hug and thumped each other on the back for good measure. As Jon turned to head back toward Burgos, I felt uneasy. The road in front of me was drab and desolate. I felt small against the vast backdrop before me, more like prey than pilgrim.

Sascha and I turned and walked together, quietly for the most part, each of us lost in thought during those first few miles. When he decided to stop for food, I forged ahead. Soon enough a tall Dutchman caught up to me. His name was Tao; he was a likeable, lanky fellow with a gentle way about him. Like a good number of Europeans I would meet during my time in Spain, he told me he had begun his pilgrimage *at his front door*, first walking from Holland to St. Jean Pied-de-Port before beginning his journey in earnest. I was flabbergasted, then impressed, and finally a bit embarrassed that the mere sight of the Meseta had cowed me. Tao's story reminded me that dreams grow as big as the dreamer allows. I jutted out my chin and steadied my nerves.

Time to face the Camino head-on.

As the terrain grew hilly, I could no longer keep up with Tao's long stride. He wished me luck and disappeared over the next peak. Once again, I was alone.

Luckily, the temperature was unusually cool that morning. Overcast skies provided me with some welcomed relief from the sun. I crisscrossed the Río Arlanzón multiple times, at one point quenching my thirst at a spring-fed fountain gushing water from four ornate spouts. The dire warnings I had heard about the Meseta's heat index were thus far unfounded.

I arrived in Hornillos just before noon, with Sascha right on my heels. The albergue was constructed of beautiful rows of stone, separated from the road by an enormous slate patio. We rambled up the steps and got our bunk assignments, a much easier task now that the size of our group had shrunk to two. Much to our delight, the bed across from mine had already been taken by James, a fellow pilgrim we had met on a number of occasions during the previous week. Originally from Louisiana, James was walking the Camino before entering the novitiate, the first step in his journey toward ordination in the Roman Catholic Church.

While we waited for Sascha to finish showering, James quizzed me on church doctrine and the theological and historical underpinnings of our shared Christian faith. He was hoping to join the Society of Jesus, more commonly known as the Jesuits.

It was the same order that produced Pope Francis. Known for their liberal tendencies, the Jesuits seemed like a good match for James. I had found a clerical soulmate, a companion of similar opinion, eager to "talk shop."

I spent the rest of the afternoon out on the terrace, writing in my journal and enjoying the occasional breeze. Every so often a pilgrim would saunter by, including my Irish friend Eileen. When she saw me, she asked where the rest of my friends had gone. "Back to the States," I replied glumly. I wonder if I looked as lonesome as I felt.

James joined Sascha and me for dinner that evening. The only bar in town was located directly across the street from the albergue. No lines, no waiting. My kind of place.

After enjoying our meal, we cut back across the patio and tucked ourselves into bed, all before 8:00 p.m. With earplugs firmly inserted, I drifted off into a dreamless slumber.

I awoke the next morning at 6:15 a.m. To my surprise, half of the bunkhouse had already left, including James. I stretched my arms over my head and gingerly got out of bed. My joints had begun to ache the day prior, despite the ace bandage I had wrapped around my balky left knee. If I didn't place my foot absolutely square on the ground, a searing pain would shoot across the back of my kneecap. I had even yelped out loud a handful of times during the previous day's hike, an involuntary reaction to the zinging stab I felt after every awkward step. Beth had left me her walking sticks when she departed, urging me to use them. While I had reluctantly agreed, I promptly lashed them to my pack, mostly because I wanted my hands to be free. Today I would give them a try. There was no point in being hardheaded about it.

During the past few days, I had walked due west, with the morning sun located directly behind me. This backlighting cast a long shadow, beginning at my feet and extending forward, making me appear as if I were 10 feet taller and 50 pounds lighter. Each morning I would "chase" that silhouette as the sun continued to rise. Soon enough, I found myself relying on its reach as a pseudo watch. When my shadow disappeared it was noon, the time I usually called it quits. Particularly on the Meseta, walking during the heat of the day was not advisable.

But that morning some thunderstorms had rolled through, leaving in their wake deep puddles and even deeper mud. Bolstered by my poles, I slogged cautiously through the molasses-like muck. At one point, the suction pulled my hiking shoe right off, forcing me to hop backward on one leg to retrieve it.

There were a number of pilgrims who had chosen to traverse the Camino by bicycle and they had it even worse that day. The mud clung to their tires and spokes, flinging watery clay onto their gear shaft and panniers with every turn of the handlebars. Every one of them eventually disembarked, hoisting their two-wheelers up onto their shoulders until they found a spot dry enough to try again. It was tough going for hiker and biker alike.

Sascha and I were delayed by our battle with the mud, and it was already midafternoon by the time we finally arrived at Castrojeriz, a village of just over 1,000 residents. We had walked 13.2 miles (21.2 km), making this the second day in a row we had kept on schedule. I was proud of this accomplishment, but my legs were battered and my pants were drenched in ooze from the trail. The host of our hostel took pity on me and graciously carried my pack up the stairs to my room. After taking a shower, I began the task of washing my clothes in the bathroom sink. By the time I finished, my bar of soap had shrunk to a sliver.

Our host's generosity extended to Sascha as well. After we had register and paid, he sweetened the deal by giving Sascha two fresh eggs, laid that morning by the family's hen. Sascha boiled and peeled them, added them to a bowl of pasta, and then seasoned the recipe with pickled tuna. It was a luxury to have my dinner made and delivered to my cot, even if it involved canned fish preserved in vinegar. Once again, I was reminded how fortunate I was to have Sascha as my partner in crime.

But not everything had gone smoothly that day. The low point had come early on, when I realized my camera battery had died. With only my memory to rely on, I made a point of walking a bit more slowly, studying every detail along the way. At the end of the afternoon, I came upon *Arco de San Antón*, a stone archway belonging to the ruins of an 11th-century monastery and hospice. Known primarily for its curative powers, the monastery had also gained notoriety for leaving loaves of bread in the small openings of the building's edifice. Hungry pilgrims throughout the ages had been the benefactors of these small acts of kindness.

Contemporary hikers followed a similar practice, sticking handwritten notes into these same cavities. As I approached the wall, it seemed like every crevice was already stuffed with a scrap of paper. Undeterred, I sat down on the side of the path and penned a note to Beth, and then another to CeCe. After finding an open spot in the crumbling mortar, I too tucked my notes into the stone.

The first, a promise. The second, a prayer.

Phantom Pain

"I've always felt that adolescence is what makes the person.
That time is the most intense, the most difficult, the most
amazing time in a person's life."

—Alice Hoffman, *The Probable Future*

My Dad used to call it phantom pain, the biting sting he would
experience in the portion of his right leg no longer there. Even
after the flesh had been removed, the nerves still remembered.

They ached for what was, before the trauma changed things
forever.

Although I was expending a good deal of mental energy
strategizing about how best to meet the physical challenges of
the Meseta, the real drain I was experiencing was emotional.
Thoughts of CeCe flooded my every waking moment. I re-played
conversations in my head, hearing her voice so clearly it was as
if she were standing right next to me. I wondered how she had
concocted her plan. What had she thought about on the return
flight after seeing her family, or how had she decided when she
was done tweaking her goodbye letters? I even got sidetracked on
nonsensical tangents like which was her favorite sweater or why

she had named her cat as she did. It was like a record I couldn't shut off, forever spinning, spinning, spinning.

The solitude, the barren landscape, and the deadening hush provided the perfect backdrop for this splatter of emotional graffiti. But it was a tapestry, and not a singular thread, that was unraveling, a storyline carefully woven years and years before CeCe and I ever met.

She wasn't the first person I knew, nor the last, to attempt suicide. Twice while I was a teenager, my only sibling tried to end his life. Although he was unsuccessful, the emotional impact of his actions still reverberates within me today. The subject remains a taboo one between us. I imagine the aftershocks linger for him as well. A scab never quite healed. A wound not able to scar.

The family secret.

When I think about it now, that time in my life is just a jumble of flashbacks. I remember my parents huddled together in disbelief after hearing the news of his first attempt, rendered both mute and inert. They looked shell-shocked actually, a reaction that surprised me. After all, my brother hadn't had an easy go of it. He had been hamstrung by significant learning disabilities, making school a torturous place for him. When you are young, the only yardstick against which you are measured is school. Which means kids who struggle in the classroom ... struggle.

In the 1960s, there was precious little understanding of decreased processing speed, executive functioning deficits, dyslexia, or ADHD. Poor grades were attributed to one thing and one thing only – a lack of effort.

My parents tried everything to pull my brother from the grip of his academic mediocrity. They cajoled. They yelled. They punished and pleaded. But nothing worked. My brother's labors still produced little fruit.

His difficulties were exacerbated by his appearance. He was always the biggest kid in the class. Already six feet tall in sixth grade, adults often thought he was much older than he was. When he displayed age-appropriate behavior, it was often mistaken as juvenile, prompting a cascade of lectures and eye rolls from the adults who surrounded him.

His growth spurts were extreme. My mother often joked he never woke up with his legs the same length as when he had gone to bed. He struggled with his ever-changing body, gangly and awkward for much of his youth. His height made it impossible for him to blend into the scenery, ever. It was an unfortunate situation that virtually guaranteed all of his shortcomings would be noticed.

To my mother's credit, she attacked this problem as she did everything else – at full throttle. She waded hip-deep into the stacks of our local library, rabid for any helpful morsel of information she could find. She read medical journals. She talked to the school personnel. And, over time, she gleaned enough data to conclude my brother's struggles were hardwired and not the by-product of his presumed laziness.

Soon I was tapped to join the support network my mother carefully designed. She tasked me with reading all of my brother's school assignments into a tape recorder. This enabled him to benefit from a multi-sensory approach to learning, simultaneously seeing *and* hearing his assignments. It was a strategy well-suited to his literature classes where the primary task was reading, and the initial results were good. But it proved to be too little too late.

By that point, he had endured years and years of frustration and the subsequent self-loathing that often follows. He had taken to heart all of the things the adults in his life had told him; that he wasn't smart enough, that he wasn't disciplined enough, that he wasn't ever going to be good enough.

His confidence level tanked. His behavioral problems became more frequent. Given how difficult adolescence already is, it seemed predestined this particular pot would boil over.

I knew everyone who struggled didn't necessarily respond in such a severe way, but I also knew my brother was fragile. His attempted suicide made this a reality we could no longer ignore.

For the rest of my teenage years, I waited for the other shoe to drop. During the first few months after his attempt, I would press my ear tightly to our shared bedroom wall at night, straining to hear a sound that would assure me he was still alive. A chair scraping the floor. The closet door opening. A muffled snore. I was scared every moment of every day. And for the first time in my life, I realized my parents were fallible. They were floundering just as much as I was, which made a frightening situation even worse.

Desperate to swing the pendulum in the other direction, I committed every ounce of energy I had to becoming the perfect child. I didn't do it consciously, but that was the end result. With so much on their plate, my parents didn't need anything else to worry about.

I excelled academically. I made varsity. I collected enough friends in "high places" to belong, however marginally, to the "cool kids" group. I did what I was told. I kept up appearances.

I was so innocuous, I all but disappeared.

But my plan backfired. My brother grew to resent my overachieving ways. The inevitable comparison between us became more and more lopsided. We were in the same grade because of the close proximity of our birthdates; that reality made the juxtapositions all the more frequent.

As time went by, he began to attribute my success to luck rather than effort. "You have it so easy," he would mutter. "The golden child, everything given to you on a silver platter."

Depending on the day, my reaction vacillated between contempt and compassion. But mostly, we existed in a space of uneasy truce.

My mother continued her tireless campaign to protect him for the remainder of her life. In those early years, my brother's reaction was predictable. He both clung to her and stiff-armed her, as most teenagers do. But as he grew older, he began to rely on her far too much. Instead of helping, her efforts became infantilizing. The disfunction was further complicated by their shared temperament, making for an often-explosive atmosphere. Like two magnets, they were tethered by an invisible force that both pulled them together and pushed them apart.

My father remained unwilling to venture out onto this emotional high wire, leaving my mother to plow ahead on her own. Not surprisingly, she grew to resent it, causing a fissure I'm not sure ever completely resolved. He didn't understand my brother, not in any sort of meaningful way, and believed his challenges could be overcome by an uptick of tenacity and pluck. Lapses in discipline of any kind did not sit well in my father's wheelhouse.

Until I left for college, I continued my "out of sight, out of mind" strategy. But even keeping a low profile seemed to annoy my mother. No doubt she was scared. Certainly frustrated. Worse yet, she often felt alone in shouldering the emotional burdens of our family. When the irritations got the best of her, she needed a target. And that target was me.

Met by her increasing ire, I retreated even further. Eventually my affect became largely one of stony silence. Every fight needed two combatants, so I simply refused to engage. I got good grades. I wrote thank you notes. I did errands for the elderly folks in the neighborhood. But I rebuffed any attempt my mother made to engage with me emotionally. When she complained I was sullen or petulant, I just shrugged.

My disdain for drama and volatility became deeply ingrained. So much so that I still struggle in situations that contain high emotional content. More than anything, the aftermath of my brother's suicide attempts taught me the benefits of controlling my emotions. Nothing good ever came from unruly behavior. The only acceptable weapon in my adolescent arsenal was silence. Often mistaken as poise, silence was the way in which I could mask my fury, or angst, or fear. Silence swaddled me in a hero's white cape; never sullied, never judged and, thankfully, never noticed.

On the Meseta, the silence was now deafening. Mile after mile, this bleak outcrop of rock was a wordless, dormant, noiseless desert. For the first time in my life, silence brought me no comfort.

Ordinary Time

A time of growth and maturation.
For those days when there is no special feast.

27

Peeling the Onion

"Books are the quietest and most constant of friends; they are the most accessible and wisest of counselors, and the most patient of teachers."

—Charles W. Eliot

As I was leaving the albergue the next morning, I was pleasantly surprised to discover James, the soon-to-be seminarian, lounging in the reception area. On the trail, his pace was quite brisk, allowing him to take plenty of detours if the mood struck him. He would often start off ahead of us, then peel off on some side trail, only to stroll in at day's end within minutes of our arrival.

James, Sascha, and I bounded down the stairs together just as the sun began to peek out from the horizon. But our exuberance didn't last for long. Just outside of town, the path merged with an old Roman road, placing us at the bottom of yet another ferocious incline. Alto Mostelares, 2,952 feet high (900 m), proved easy enough for James, the human mountain goat. He bolted while I plodded. By the time I reached the top, both he and Sascha had disappeared from view.

Despite the challenging start, I rolled into Boadvilla, just over 12 miles (20 km) into the day's itinerary, still feeling pretty good. Buoyed by a new-found confidence, Sascha and I decided to continue on to Frómista, extending our hike another 3 miles (5 km). We had never gone off script and increased our mileage tally on the fly. I hoped we wouldn't regret doing so now.

The scenery that day was mesmerizing, and the sheer beauty of it helped distract me from the strain of walking the appendaged distance. The route hugged a broad and tranquil canal. As I strolled along, the slow-moving water seemed to keep pace, luring me forward.

We caught another break when we discovered the municipal albergue was located on the front edge of town, unexpectedly shortening our day. After checking in, I crawled into my bunk for a much-needed siesta. It was the third day in a row we had kept on task. Three days. Forty-two miles (67.5 km).

That night, as we were lounging around a long wooden table in the hostel's main entryway, James came in hobbling. Leaning heavily on a crutch, he shifted his weight quickly off his sore foot. Sascha and I sprang to our feet and linked our arms under both of his shoulders. Now stationed on either side, we gently padded across the floor, lowering him into a cushioned chair. With pain running the full length of his right leg, James looked miserable and felt even worse. He had already decided he would stay an extra day to rest. By the looks of him, I wasn't sure that would be enough.

We struck out on the early side the following morning, waking James briefly to say goodbye. Given the extent of his injury, I thought there was a good chance we wouldn't see him again. Carrión de los Condes was the yardstick marker for the day, a walk of just 12.2 miles (19.7 km). Without a hill in sight, I felt an extra giddy-up in my step. Unfortunately, my exuberance was short-lived.

The sun was relentless that morning. Worse yet, there was no escaping it. Streams of sweat ran down my face and neck, stretching the collar of my cotton t-shirt. The damp fabric clung to my stomach and back. Even my socks began to feel moist.

Pungent with perspiration, I soon attracted a horde of gnats. The cloud of bugs spent the rest of the day gleefully circling my head, an infuriating irritant that quickly got under my skin. Out of the corner of my eye, I saw a pilgrim on horseback. She had thoughtfully placed some netting on her steed's head, protecting his eyes from the day's onslaught of insects. Unprepared for such a circumstance, I spent the morning furiously swatting at the air.

Scorecard. Gnats 1. Me 0.

Just when I thought it couldn't get any worse, I felt a blister starting to form. I took off my shoe and discovered a tiny bubble had developed on my right heel, one of the few spots I hadn't covered in duct tape. I had gone 14 days without any sort of abrasion on my feet, a bit of a record in my current circle of comrades. That streak was officially over.

Luckily, Sascha was behind me and trotted over after rounding the corner. He dug through his pack and found a piece of moleskin in a side pocket. I did a quick patch job, pulled my sock on, and delicately stepped back onto the path. Having a short day on the schedule had come at just the right moment.

Carrión was a fairly large town, and one that attracted a good number of pilgrims each night. We waited in line for 45 minutes before being ushered into the hostel. Alongside us were the "Dread Sibs," a team consisting of one brother and two sisters, each sporting the most beautiful braids. Their hair was the least of it. Every time I saw them, they were adorned with different accessories. That particular day they were wearing pink sunglasses with a peace sign affixed to each lens. When they finally reached the check-in table, they were turned away. No room in the inn, they were told. Despite the refusal, they glided out of the albergue as if they didn't have a care in the world. I remember thinking maybe there really was something to wearing "rose-colored glasses."

The end of the day was marked by two of my favorite things – Fanta and nuns.

The soda came courtesy of a nearby internet café we happened upon. Once at the counter, I pointed to the biggest cup in the display and then motioned to a sign advertising my best-loved soda. The barista smiled and nodded. With drink in hand, I basked in its fizzy deliciousness, slurping it down in huge cold gulps. But it would be the nuns who would rule the night.

After dinner, the sisters running our albergue gathered us together for a bit of storytelling and singing. Sascha was goaded into performing a solo and dazzled the room with his rich baritone voice. When he finished, the group erupted in applause. It was his own American Idol moment, and a well-deserved one at that.

Then one of the nuns told what she called the "onion story." She spoke of an enchanted place filled with jewels, each one bright with color and sparkle. But despite their beauty, the jewels were rebuked by those around them. Each was warned it must give up its twinkle, lest it appear too boastful or haughty. No member of the community was allowed to be different, not if a peaceful co-existence was to be maintained. So, the jewels covered themselves in drab and dingy attire, trading their shiny allure for the safety inherent in being part of the crowd.

The story went on to reveal that the jewels were later discovered by the town elder. When they told him of their predicament, he convinced them not to be swayed by the opinions of those around them. Slowly the jewels began to discard the layers under which they had been hiding. He was so moved by their courage, the elder began to cry. And so began the practice of weeping every time an onion was peeled; a reminder of the veiled beauty that lay just below the surface.

I was struck by the poignancy and insight of the nun's parable. Assimilation, purely to gain the protection it afforded, was a battle I had lost more frequently than I cared to admit. This was yet another reminder to me of the importance of internalizing my "let go" mantra.

At the end of our time together, the sisters gave each of us a star made from pieces of decorative paper. They told us the gift would help illuminate our passage to Santiago. As the evening drew to a close, they prayed for our safe passage, they prayed for our discernment, and they prayed each of us would shed whatever layers were shielding our tender hearts. "Be the onion," they urged us. I couldn't imagine a better blessing.

That night, just before I slipped into my sleeping bag, I discovered a book. It had been left on a side table in the hostel's common room. Picking it up, I saw it was written by famed veterinarian-turned-writer James Herriot. I asked around but no one else claimed it. I snatched it for myself and, after settling down in my bunk, cracked open the cover. For the first time in weeks, I turned page after page, each more luscious than the last.

The bottle of Fanta? Fabulous. The gaggle of nuns? Heartwarming. But a *book*? It was a grace beyond measure. And just like the onion, it brought tears to my eyes.

But this time, tears of joy.

The Griddle

"To live is to suffer, to survive is to find some meaning
in the suffering."

—Friedrich Nietzsche

It was a fitful sleep that night as the darkness was regularly
pierced by cheering Spaniards, victors once again in the World
Cup competition, this time over neighboring Portugal.

I lumbered out of bed at daybreak and began walking the
most lifeless section of the Camino I had yet experienced. The
road was straight. Straight as an arrow. So straight I strained
to see any variation in the landscape ahead of me. Pythagoras
himself could not have convinced me the world was round that
morning. I felt like I was on a giant griddle, sizzling under the
sun, striding across an endless pancake of dirt.

The Mesata's extreme heat and lack of shade were beginning
to take their toll. An amalgamation of a bevy of recessive genes,
I had auburn hair, green eyes, and skin so fair it began to redden
within minutes of being out in the sun. In an attempt to combat
this pedigree, I had chosen to don both pants and long-sleeve
shirts for the entire time I was on the Camino, regardless of
how high the temperature rose. The only skin that ever saw the

light of day was on the back of my hands and the tips of my ears. Every morning I made sure the rest of my head and neck were shrouded under a ballcap, bandana, and a healthy dose of sunblock.

Despite my efforts, the power of the sun overwhelmed me. Small blisters began to form on the small patches of skin that were exposed, extending past my knuckles toward the tops of my fingers. With my hands now swollen and pink, it became painful to make a fist or even tie my shoes. As I walked, I could literally feel my skin burning. Occasionally I would tug my shirtsleeves down over my hands. But without being able to grasp the fabric for long, the cuffs would eventually creep back up, once again leaving the back of my hands uncovered.

By this point, the pilgrimage had become a grind. The heat. The insects. And a swath of blisters on both my hands and feet. Even the flat terrain sparked no gratitude in me. I had lost my rhythm and, in some ways, my purpose. My mental discipline was beginning to falter.

It is discouraging, and humbling, to realize the impact a bit of discomfort can provoke. I reminded myself the Camino was a marathon and not a sprint. Just keep fighting, I chanted. Just keep moving.

We stopped for the night in Caldadilla de la Cueza, at a hostel located right on the path. With another 11 miles or so (17.5 km) behind us, I was eager to spend the afternoon inside the cool interior. Paco, our host for the night, led us to a back room and then promptly chastised Sascha for throwing his pack on the lower bunk. "Those are reserved for the old and the infirm," he declared. Without missing a beat, he turned and graciously offered the cot to me. I guess it was time to stop taking myself so seriously.

Although spartan, our accommodations sported both a clothesline and a small swimming pool. After washing my clothes in the sink, I clipped them to the line stretched taut across the backyard. They dried almost immediately, baking under the heat of the sun just as I had.

With my chores now complete, I headed toward the pool. As I dipped my feet into the cool water, my skin prickled with goosebumps. It wasn't a mirage after all, I dreamily concurred.

I had found heaven.

The following day, the calendar turned to July. Clouds hovered over the trail as we exited the hostel, providing some much-appreciated shade. Sascha stopped for coffee, so I continued on by myself. A small store came into view. I rambled in and grabbed a croissant and Coke before sitting down outside. I pressed my back against a stone wall and slid my pack under both knees, converting it momentarily to my version of a Camino La-Z Boy.

I made a point of not looking at my guidebook or strategizing about the remainder of the day's hike. That was my usual modus operandi. Instead, I just enjoyed my breakfast while gazing out at the wide expanse of land in front of me. As my heart rate slowed, I could feel myself begin to relax. And then SPLAT! I turned my head and watched as the watery excrement of an overhead bird dripped down my left shoulder. *Buen Camino.*

The next stretch was a good deal warmer as the sun fought its way through the lingering morning haze. Despite my latest bout of excessive sweating, the gnats chose the sweet honeysuckle that lined the sides of the trail over me. That said, challenges still remained. The roadway was covered in loose gravel that slowed our progress considerably. By the end of the day, we rolled into Sahagún, 14 miles (22.4 km) from our starting point. I counted that as a win.

The municipal hostel was located a tad past the bullring and grain silos that marked the town's border. But the most noticeable identifier of Sahagún was its ecclesiastical architecture.

During the Middle Ages, Sahagún had played an important role in the spread of Christianity. Monasteries and chapels were stationed at nearly every corner. Even our albergue was a former church, with mattresses stuffed into various wooden cubbies of the now-defunct Iglesia de la Trinidad. Sturdy brick walls propped up the vaulted arches. The broken shards of stone and stained glass didn't negate the overall effect. It was stunning.

Jane, a 40-ish woman from Britain, arrived just after the hostel opened. We had met during an earlier portion of the trip. Like most solo hikers, she was eager to socialize. We chatted briefly while waiting for a shower to open up, both turning a bit queasy when we discovered clumps of small bugs clinging to the creases in the tiled floor. I took the fastest shower of my life that day.

While Jane and Sascha continued to banter, I sprawled across the bed and finished reading my Herriot book. Afterwards, I left it on a table in the hostel's entryway, just as had been done for me. Later that night, I saw Jane had discovered the text and had tucked it into the top pocket of her pack. As it turned out, she was a huge animal lover and had long loved the assorted tales of her veterinarian countryman. She told me the enormous nests we so often passed were those of storks, kept company by a steady stream of diving and swirling swallows. While I was impressed with her knowledge of ornithology, perhaps entomology might have been more useful.

In the continuing war between me and the bugs, the bugs were winning.

Flea Bites

"Life begins at the end of your comfort zone."

—Lionel Ritchie, *American Idol*

How do you spell flea? Y-U-C-K.

How I yearned for some good old-fashioned American cleanliness. Feeling like the 10 plagues of Exodus (*New Revised Standard Version*, chapters 7-11) were descending on me, I was desperate to escape my grungy surroundings. The never-ending presence of sweat, bugs, dirt, shared beds, and sink-washed clothes had left me feeling perpetually grimy. But on this night, I took that feeling to an entirely new level.

After arriving at the albergue of El Burgo Ranero (the town of frogs), Sascha made his way over to the only two remaining bunks in the place. The top cot was right at eye level. As he approached, he noticed something move out of the corner of his eye. He motioned me over, and taking a coin from his pocket, slowly slid it across the mattress toward the unsuspecting bug. When it got close, the insect jumped, confirming its identity as a flea.

Without an alternative at hand, we had to make the best of a bad situation. That evening I went outside to open my pack, retrieving only my toothbrush and toothpaste. I decided not to open my bag once back inside the building, hoping that would stop any bugs from catching a ride with me after our night in "Frog Town" was over. That night, instead of showering, I got into my sleeping bag with all my clothes on, including my long-sleeve shirt, pants, and socks. I tied my bandana around my mouth and neck and put my winter hat on, all despite the toasty temperature. I wanted as little skin showing as possible. Then I shut my eyes and waited for morning to come.

If I ended up covered in flea bites, at least I was going to make them work for it.

Earlier that afternoon we had visited the village church, Parroa de San Pedro. It was magnificent, with gleaming hardwood floors and sparkling white walls. Unlike so many of the musty and dim churches we had toured on the trip, this chapel was a breath of fresh air. We eagerly soaked in all of its immaculate and spotless mojo.

Looking for a new activity to amuse us, Sascha decided it was a good time to craft a Camino "like/dislike" list of our experiences to date. As he sat quietly in a pew scribbling, I did the same. When he was finished, his collection of likes was more than double that of his dislikes. Pretty remarkable, given he was about to sleep in a flea-infested bed. Mine was a bit more evenly distributed. But still, a solid approval rating for our great adventure.

Likes:
1. The lack of other Americans.
2. Meeting pilgrims from all over the world.
3. Enjoying a siesta after a day of walking.
4. Feeling physically safe, even in the most rural of areas.
5. Decreased levels of anxiety.
6. Enjoying time walking by myself.

7. Stork nests!
8. Being in Spain during the World Cup.
9. Recognizing the sensation of feeling hungry.
10. Realizing that Sascha, Jess, Meredith, and Beth had all made significant sacrifices to accompany me on this trip.

Dislikes:
1. Constantly being dirty.
2. The exhausting and penetrating heat.
3. Not having enough to read.
4. The Spanish penchant for pork and eating dinner after 8:00 p.m.
5. Being away when CeCe died.

We were roughly 225 miles (362 km) shy of Santiago. We had reached the midway point of our journey. Why did it feel like I was just getting started?

Cage or Leash?

"Such a gender line ... helps to keep women
not on a pedestal, but in a cage."

—Ruth Bader Ginsburg,
Weinberger v. Wiesenfeld, January 20, 1975

Before my mother met my father, she got a dog – an infinitely patient and well-behaved Irish terrier she named Ted. The chances that her soon-to-be boyfriend and eventual husband would also be named Ted were infinitesimally small. But there you have it. A woman and her two redheaded sidekicks, Ted and ... Ted.

After my parents got married, the threesome moved into one of those small ranch houses that sprouted like weeds after the war. Having the men in her life share the same name quickly moved from cheesy to annoying. In time, my mother tweaked the dog's name and began calling him "Teddo." He was a quick study and soon responded when called by his new moniker.

Before the advent of playdates and helicopter parents, growing up was a lot less structured and definitely less complicated. Case in point, my babysitter as a toddler was often Teddo. My mother would put my brother and me down on a shaded stripe of grass in the backyard and then return to the kitchen sink to wash dishes or start dinner. Knowing his role, Teddo would scoot through the opened screen door as my mother made her way back into the house, trotting over to where we had just been placed.

We paid him no mind of course. This was a familiar routine to us. We were focused instead on finding a stick to throw, or a clover to pick or, once we learned to stand, teetering precariously on our chubby legs like mini Frankensteins.

Teddo, guided by his herding instinct, would delineate our play space by slowly circling us. If we strayed too close to the perimeter, he would saunter over and gently nudge us in the chest with his nose. Our knees would then buckle, landing us with a thud onto our diapered bottoms. Returning to our feet, we would often attempt to continue in the same direction only to be re-directed by Teddo once again. When at last we tired of this routine, we would turn and head back toward the middle of circle, prompting him to lie down and wait until the next time we wandered too far.

My mother would peer through the kitchen window to check on us. But only the sight of blood sent her scampering back out into the yard. Otherwise, we were allowed to explore and experience and settle our differences without the lurking presence of our parents.

Watched without interference, we were safe but not protected. Looking back, I wonder if part of my appetite for travel was sown in those nascent days. Having a bit of slack in your leash can do that to a person.

This theme would continue as we grew older. My parents didn't entertain us as so many parents do nowadays. If we wanted to spend time with them, we did what *they* did. Maybe that was running errands in the car with my mother. Maybe that was handing my Dad some tools while he tinkered with a project. We were given plenty of time to play with the assorted ruffians who populated our neighborhood, riding bikes and slinging baseballs. But our parents were *our parents*, and not our friends.

Little did I know what an enormous impact this distinction would make.

Even more formative was my father's wartime injury, in so many ways the catalyst to my own interest in leading an adventuresome life. The 1960s, until the tumultuous later years of the decade, were in many ways akin to the 1950s. Men went to work. Women stayed at home. Families ate supper together every evening and driveways were filled with Oldsmobiles. At least that was the case in my neighborhood.

There were precious few situations where gender norms were allowed to blur. Earning salaries, doing yardwork, and repairing the car all fell under the exclusive purview of men. And there they stayed.

But my father's disability meant many of these chores were beyond his capabilities. He couldn't climb a ladder. He couldn't walk behind a lawnmower. He couldn't crawl into a tight space to adjust a pipe or run new wiring. Which meant I did.

My brother, never one for detailed work, was quickly forgiven of these tasks. When the need arose to tackle a project that required precision and patience, like painting woodwork or trimming hedges, I was the one my father tapped. It was not only that I was nimble and attentive to the work. I was also much smaller than my Dad, more easily able to angle a socket wrench into a tight space or squeeze beneath the undercarriage of the car. Things like changing the oil or loosening the trap of the bathroom sink became mine to do, always under my father's watchful eye.

Hour after hour, my father taught me how to do the things he could no longer do. In the process, I learned the mechanics of most household machinery. I could easily identify a wide array of tools. I grew to love working with my hands and enjoyed the satisfaction of a job well done.

This was a significant departure from the experiences of every other girl on my street. They were relegated to the same roles as were their mothers; setting the table each evening and helping with the laundry. The few tomboys in the vicinity mixed it up with the boys on the playground. But when dinnertime rolled around, it was back inside the house, even for them.

Patent leather shoes were the norm for Sundays. Dresses were donned for the school picture. The adults in my neighborhood spent a tremendous amount of time teaching the girls how to behave like "young ladies." Emphasis on behave.

Despite being immersed in this culture, I was also removed from it. Even more surprising, not a single negative comment came my way regarding my dalliance from the standard protocol of the time. I was given a pass for my unorthodox upbringing because my father was a decorated war hero. Out of deference to and respect for his sacrifice, I was allowed to paint outside the lines because, in doing so, I was helping *him*. Not only was I permitted to embody this gender-bending role, I was lauded for it. Instead of being seen as an upstart, bucking the conventions of the time, I was praised for being a dutiful daughter.

In addition to having so much more freedom than the other girls around me, I was constantly reminded how capable I was. As a result, I grew to trust my body rather than critique it. I wasn't taught to "perform" for men by being cute, or feigning knowledge, or courting compliments. I was praised instead for problem solving and self-reliance. It never occurred to me that I was too delicate, physically or emotionally, to tackle difficult challenges. With no fences erected to contain my ambition, the underlying message was clear. Anything was possible if I dedicated myself completely to the task at hand.

My father, a man's man and in many ways a traditionalist, changed when he had a daughter. My mother surely added fuel to the fire in this regard. Her atypical and strident persona wasn't the norm for the time either. But the thought that his own child should be hindered by something as arbitrary as her chromosomes was inconceivable to him. No one was going to cage me. No one.

The explosion of a grenade, thrown almost 20 years before my birth, would shatter *my* world as well as my father's. But he made sure his loss was my gain.

The Stalker

"Being alone is scary, but not as scary as feeling alone."

—Amelia Earhart

In the morning, I strolled past the infamous pond where the town's frogs supposedly convened. I bid them adieu with no love lost. In my estimation, they had clearly shirked their duties. Flies and fleas were ubiquitous in El Burgo Ranero. The frogs had either left town or lost their appetites.

Whatever the reason, I had taken it on the chin. The fleas had had their way with me the previous night. I was itchy from head to toe.

Nonetheless, the hamlet still had its charms. Sascha and I added two new members to our pilgrimage tribe – Frankie and Patrick. Tall, blond, and lanky, both hailed from Germany and were on an extended holiday. Patrick was soon to begin a program in social work. Frankie had just left his teaching job and was moving to Munich. With new-found time on their hands, they decided to give the Camino a go.

All of us had been crossing paths for a stretch of time by then, waving occasionally or stopping for a quick chat, but never together at day's end. A group of boisterous Italians had commandeered the hostel's kitchen that night, forcing the rest of us outside to the wooden benches in the yard. When Sascha and I popped out of the side door of the albergue, there they were. We plopped down beside them and passed a bottle of wine between us, jabbering between sips. Within a half an hour, Eileen walked by. We motioned her over and she joined our drinking circle. I learned she too was a teacher on holiday, enjoying a respite from her math and geography students. Before hoisting her pack back on, she let me know Evelyn was just a short bit behind us. It was likely we would see her sometime during the next day's hike.

The development of this web of friendships was fast becoming the cornerstone of my Camino experience. Even if the partnerships were fleeting, these transient moments provided companionship and an opportunity to indulge my most pressing curiosity. Why were so many drawn to this experience? What was it that had captured their imaginations and brought them to this desolate outpost? And if we did stumble across the answer, would we even know?

No matter the result, and despite vast differences in age, nationality, and personal perspective, my fellow hikers became soulmates of a sort during our time together, bonded by our shared experience. I remember thinking what a different world it would be if all of us could cultivate this kind of instantaneous kinship outside of the Camino.

The next morning, our path consisted of a gentle downward slope all the way to Mansilla de las Mulas, named in part for its livestock industry. Although the day's journey covered 15.2 miles (24.5 km), we rambled into town quite early. It was a relief to finally have such an easy patch of terrain to traverse.

Smack dab in the middle of town was a beautiful albergue, adorned with sturdy wooden steps and private showers. Eileen, Patrick, and Frankie were all sitting on the front stoop when we arrived. Thrilled to be back with the crew, we decided to share a large room that night. Evelyn strolled into town just a few hours later. She squeezed into a bunk beside me for the night, rounding out our group quite nicely.

The last time I had shared sleeping quarters with Evelyn, she had stumbled into the hostel at Santo Domingo after consuming the lion's share of a jug of wine. Beth and I jumped out of our bunks in an effort to corral her, but it wasn't easy. After a good deal of wrangling, we managed to untie her boots and remove her shirt and pants before pouring her into her sleeping bag. But not before waking up many of our fellow pilgrims and flashing a good deal of skin.

The next morning, Beth and I had a laugh about the previous night's hijinks. Poor Evelyn didn't share our amusement. Holding her aching head in her hands, she started the day by swallowing a handful of aspirin and praying for relief.

This time around was much tamer. The group meandered over to a nearby café for dinner. Its outdoor patio was covered in trellised grapevines. I sat next to Eileen and she told me stories of what it was like to grow up in Cork. I was fascinated to learn she had a transgender sibling. We talked at length about the ways in which this affected her and the other members of her family. There was something so genuine and kind about her. It was a lovely end to a lovely day.

After our meal, Eileen and some of the group went to a bar to watch the remainder of the soccer game while I returned to the albergue. Before too long, cheers shook the walls. With another win under her belt, Spain was headed to the semi-finals to face Germany. World Cup fever continued on.

Our hike across the final portion of the Meseta fell fittingly on July 4th, my long-awaited "Independence Day" from its stifling heat. But despite the relatively modest mileage (11.6

m/18.6 km) that lay ahead, the Meseta found a way to deliver a few final whacks.

With Alto del Portillo (900 m) between us and León, Sascha and I decided we would each walk at our own pace. In other words, alone. We agreed to meet at the Plaza Regal, a vast expanse of stone surrounding the city's majestic medieval cathedral.

Leaning forward stiffly, I climbed uphill for nearly 3 miles (5 km) before reaching the summit. This punishing ascent made my legs feel like jelly. This was particularly problematic considering I needed to cross a highway once at the top, dodging cars with video game agility. Once on the other side, I entered the gritty fringe of León, walking on a street that ran parallel to the congested N-601. The pavement was tough on my knees, which distracted me enough that, for the first time on the Camino, I lost track of the yellow slashes of paint that marked the trail. As a result, I wandered into a less than desirable neighborhood. I had gotten myself pretty turned around. It was unnerving.

In my peripheral vision, I noticed a man had begun to follow me. He looked disheveled. Perhaps homeless. Perhaps just down on his luck. Whatever the case, when I began to walk faster, he too picked up the pace. I quickly scanned the block ahead and saw that the remainder of the street was deserted. This was going to be tricky.

As he got closer, I considered my options. Running was out of the question. My pack was heavy and, even without my pack, I didn't think I had the energy to create any real distance between us. I didn't have anything of real value. He likely had figured that out just by looking at me. Without a wad of cash to hand over nor the ability to flee, I determined I had no other recourse. If confronted, I would fight.

I slowed my pace ever so slightly. Sure enough, the distance between us began to shrink. Once the gap closed to within 10 feet I spun sharply, slipping off my pack in one fluid motion, and began screaming at the top of my lungs. I flailed my arms furiously. I didn't care if he thought I had become unhinged. I was ready to go down swinging.

At first, he retreated, startled by my sudden eruption. He didn't say anything but he didn't leave either. He just stared, perplexed but unfazed. I continued my tirade while he stood motionless. After a minute or so I reached down and retrieved my pack. As I backed away, he continued to follow me, but this time, a bit further behind.

When I finally crossed a street where a handful of people were lingering, I approached a woman walking a small dog and asked if she could point me toward the cathedral. She couldn't make heads or tails of my Spanish, but another woman walking by chirped in broken English that she could take me there. Without a second thought, I got into her white Renault and closed the door swiftly behind me. As we pulled away from the curb, I watched as the image of my follower disappeared from view.

She drove through a maze of streets and then deposited me at the appointed plaza, discreetly opening her window during the drive to allow for an influx of fresh air. I was soaked in sweat by that point, sweat created from exertion and sweat distilled by fear. It was a potent combination.

When she pulled up to the curb, I thanked her profusely and crawled out of the front seat. As I started across the plaza, I saw Evelyn. We hugged as I told her of my frightening encounter. Within minutes, Sascha arrived at the steps of the church. Happy to be back together, the three of us sat down on the warm stones, thighs pressed up against one another. Wedged safely between them, I finally exhaled.

After some time went by, we were approached by a young couple on their honeymoon. They had come to León as a jumping off point for a few days of hiking. We told them of our experiences of the Camino, skipping over the events of the past hour or so. Their enthusiasm was so unbridled they practically glowed.

In turn, they recommended a quirky boutique hotel, located on the edge of the stone patio. Months ago, when I had originally planned our itinerary, I had added in a day here and there to rest and recover. León had been designated as one such spot. Besides, spending an extra night in a hotel sounded positively decadent at that juncture. We were sold. Wishing the newlyweds well, we headed off to find the Hotel Albany.

Just as they assured us, it was right around the corner. Sleek in that Scandinavian kind of way, it was a feast for the eyes and, as it turned out, easy on the wallet. We paid to hold our spot. While waiting for our room to be cleaned, we headed back to the Cathedral to attend midday Mass.

By the time we returned, the needed preparations were complete. Room key in hand, we made our way to the appointed door. As the lock clicked open, we entered what would be our home for the next two nights.

It was immaculate. The sheets were white and taut. The sink and shower tiles gleamed. A soft breeze wafted through the slats of the window. I suddenly felt like I had landed on the moon. The décor was both sterile and foreign, and nothing could have made me happier.

For a moment Sascha and I just stared, not wanting to disturb the quiet luxury of it all. I felt a smile creep across my face. We were going to sleep like the dead.

After taking long and insanely hot showers, we collapsed onto our beds. Sascha fell asleep as soon as his head hit the pillow. I took the opportunity to turn on the television and watch Rafael Nadal win his second Wimbledon championship, perfunctorily dispatching his foe in straight sets. The Spaniards really were on a roll that summer.

I roused Sascha after the match was over and we made our way to a local restaurant. We were hellbent on eating as much spaghetti and buttered bread as humanly possible. Afterwards, bloated but unrepentant, we took advantage of a local WIFI connection and sent a video message to Beth before returning to the hotel.

I closed my eyes knowing I could sleep as long as I wanted – an uncommon indulgence. As I nestled my head onto the corner of the feather pillow, I detected the faintest hint of bleach. It was as if I had died and gone straight to heaven.

The next day was largely spent running errands. I bought a new charger for my camera battery. We exchanged some money. I scrubbed all of my clothes and then celebrated by taking an extended nap. Then I spent the remainder of the afternoon sitting in the sun writing postcards. Wanting to mail them before our departure, I headed into the cathedral's museum hoping to purchase a few stamps. Who was on his way out as I was on my way in?

Our old friend James.

Over dinner that night, he told us of his latest health challenges. He had injured a tendon in his foot, a condition that worsened with each day of hiking. By that point, he was limping badly.

He had tried to walk to León but couldn't manage it. Forced to take a bus to the cathedral, James was already resigned to continuing his ride all the way to Astorga, another 30 or so miles west of León. He would stop there to see a museum before taking the bus to Sarria, located just 73 miles (117 km) east of Santiago.

Sarria, perhaps more than any other locale on the Camino besides Santiago, plays a critical role for those traversing the trail. To be considered a true pilgrim, and therefore eligible to receive a Compostela, each hiker must walk at least the last 100 km of the route. As a result, almost everyone begins their pilgrimage there, the closest point that still allows for a certificate to be conferred. At the very least, James was determined to do this. He had traversed large chunks of the pilgrimage prior to this, so reaching the cumulative mileage total wasn't the problem. But without walking this last stretch, he knew his effort would be rendered illegitimate. He vowed he would make it to Santiago, even if he had to crawl.

But mostly we talked about other things during our time together that evening. It was a languid night, filled with heaps of food and glasses sloshing with wine. Our fondness for one another was evident, developed over the many miles we had shared. We lingered once our meal was done, not wanting our time together to end. After a long hug, Sascha and I said goodbye to James and watched him recede into the darkness. I knew it would be the last time we would see him, or any of our old crew for that matter. Jess, Meredith, and Beth had left in Burgos. Chicago, Dublin, Eileen, Evelyn, and now James had passed us. Perhaps the Camino would proffer new companions on the road ahead. Perhaps not. Either way, the final leg was upon us.

It was Santiago or bust.

Shaman's Magic

"What people resist the most about spiritual healing is changing their minds."

—S. Kelley Harrell

We set the alarm that night, wanting to get an early start. At 6:15 a.m., we hit the road. It was quiet except for the rustle of a stray piece of trash tumbling across the street and the occasional bark of a dog. The only movement I saw was that of other pilgrims, fleeting shadows sliding down the narrow road ahead of me.

Our original plan was to walk to Mazarife, nearly 14.5 miles (23.1 km) west of the city's center. In the dim morning light, it was difficult to spot the scallop shells that marked the trail, particularly in the industrial neighborhoods in which we found ourselves. Further complicating things was the presence of two major forks on the day's route, each offering alternative paths to the main trail. The two variations covered the same distance, but ended at different locations. Determined not to become untethered from one another, Sascha and I agreed to stop when we arrived at the first fork and wait for the other, no matter how long it might take. Once together, we would then decide which way to go, based on our remaining stamina, the weather, and the terrain ahead.

The first "Y" came at La Virgen del Camino, the last outpost of the busy suburbs of León. We had walked 5.5 miles (8.9 km) at that juncture. In the process, we had crossed the Río Bernesga, a set of railroad tracks, and climbed 328 feet (100 m) in elevation. Despite even hillier territory ahead, we chose to veer right at this first break, alleviating our need to stop again at the second fork, a split that would have been part of the itinerary had we gone left.

For the remainder of the day, our chosen course ran alongside the noisy N-120. The roar of the traffic was deafening, and yet I enjoyed the walk. I felt physically stronger than I had in quite some time. Having an extra day of rest had clearly made a difference.

In the early afternoon, I came across a long cement tunnel that extended beneath a grassy hill. There was no way to avoid it and remain on the trail. As I entered my eyes were still adjusting to the change in light when, in the distance, I heard a lone male voice echoing in the chamber. My nerves jangled, clearly still on edge from my disquieting interaction on the other side of León. The idea of being trapped in a concrete pipe with some man I didn't know unglued me. I stopped, straining to catch any other sound. The only thing I could see was a small spot of light at the end of the tunnel. Hearing nothing further, I willed my feet to move cautiously, but deliberately, into the darkness.

When I emerged at the other end, I saw a man – presumably the same man whose voice I had heard earlier – standing beside two women who were adjusting bandages on their feet. He was middle-aged, with a bit of a paunch and a receding hairline. For all I knew he could have been the nicest of guys, surrounded by the trappings of his station in life, including a gaggle of grandchildren and the bad back to go along with it. But when you live in a woman's body, you never know. You never know what will be safe and what will not. It is exhausting and demoralizing and, frankly, an infuriating way to live.

I remember many years ago trying to explain to my gentle but towering and broad-shouldered brother that the women who occupied the sidewalk alongside him at dusk, or those walking to their car in a desolate parking garage, might be afraid of him. I encouraged him to quell their apprehensions by purposely taking a more circuitous route, far-reaching enough so they would recognize he wasn't a threat.

"But I would never hurt anyone," he earnestly lamented.

"I believe you," I replied. "But that's not the point. Women are not mind readers. They don't know what you're thinking or what you might do." He returned my comment with a look of such confusion I realized it might not be possible for him to understand, at the deepest level, what it was like to inhabit the body of the "fairer sex." But it's a burden every woman lives with, no matter how much she might wish she didn't.

The rest of the day's journey came and went without incident. That night we stayed at a converted schoolhouse in Villadangos del Páramo. The albergue was set back from the road, buffered by a lush patch of lawn. There were 80 beds inside, providing respite for plenty of weary pilgrims. But in order to maximize their number, the cots were arranged with just a sliver of space between them. We were packed in like sardines.

The person in the bunk next to me was significantly overweight, his feet swelled by edema. While his legs surely benefitted from being raised up off the floor, he could scarcely breathe once prone. His airway became so depressed, he spent half the night panting and the other half snoring. Worse yet, he didn't really fit on his mattress. Folds of flesh spilled over the sides of the slim bedframe. There were many points during the evening when I awoke to his arm or hand pushing up against me.

In an effort to escape his meaty grasp, I hugged the far side of my own cot, tucking my hand between the mattress and metal frame and then curling my fingers around the coils. Holding on tightly kept me from inadvertently migrating back toward the center of my bed.

I must have dozed off at some point because, when I opened my eyes at 6:00 a.m., Sascha and I were the only ones left in the hostel. We gathered our gear and started the day by walking the gravel path headed out of town. Eager to get going, Sascha quickly disappeared from view. Just as quickly, the trail ahead of me veered off into some high grass. A few minutes later, I was waist high in a tangle of vines, weeds, and undergrowth. Had I taken a wrong turn? It sure seemed like it. But I was loathe to go backwards, so I continued to hack my way through the brush for almost 8 miles (12.5 km) before reaching the quaint village of Hospital de Órbigo. Once I crossed the river by way of a stunning medieval stone bridge, my relief was palpable.

Sascha was waiting for me at a small café, situated on a lovely deck overlooking the water. During breakfast, we squinted at the map in the guidebook before selecting Santibañez de Valdeiglesia as our stopping point for the night. We settled the bill, pushed back from the table, and once again began to walk.

At the edge of town, the path split again. A local woman explained if we headed directly to Santibañez we would have to climb a very steep hill. If we chose the alternate route, it would be longer but flatter. We could avoid the hill by extending our walk to Astorga, tagging on an additional 9.1 miles (14.7 km) to our day. Either that, or we'd have to hoof it up the hill.

As we debated between our two choices, it occurred to me that we might be headed toward an impending disaster. Having slashed my way through the first 8 miles of the day, I wasn't eager to follow that with a thigh-burning mountain climb. But selecting the other route would push our cumulative total for the day to 17.1 miles (27.5 km). With no albergues or sources of food along the way, this was the "do or die" option. We picked "long but flat," hoping for the best.

We also had enough common sense to craft a contingency plan. A few kilometers up the road there was a cut-through that doubled back to Santibañez. Sascha and I agreed to stop at that intersection in case we needed to revise our plan. Off we went.

As promised, the fork soon emerged. Drained by the heat, we decided a more conservative strategy was best and turned again toward Santibañez. This necessitated a return to the hills the following day. Neither of us had the mettle to continue to Astorga with the sun at its apex, even with the promise of a more forgiving path. We would stay put and try again in the morning.

The only available albergue that night was decidedly on the dingy side. Flies slowly buzzed in circles over our heads. Every surface was streaked with grime. Turning a blind eye to the tattered bed linens, I keeled over onto the nearest bunk. Fatigue had rendered me devoid of any kind of hygienic standards. I was exhausted.

An hour later, I returned to a bench outside, journal in hand. Unfortunately, there was no respite from the heat that day. Even while sitting still, I was drenched in sweat. A wave of discouragement washed over me. When was this going to get easier?

I was distracted from my pity party when a fellow pilgrim wandered by, a Latvian, headed in the other direction. In all my time on the Camino, I had never seen anyone walking the other way, back toward France. This was expressly designed as a one-way journey. Curiosity got the best of me and I called out to him.

I set my journal and pen aside and tapped the bench seat beside me. He sat down and began to regale me with a rather fantastical story. For the past four years, he had been walking the Camino. If he needed a break, he would volunteer at an albergue for a stretch. Just long enough to get the itch again. He was in no rush. He wasn't headed anywhere in particular. He just wanted to keep walking, watching the world go by at whatever pace he chose.

When our conversation came to a lull, he took the opportunity to get up and wander over to a nearby fountain. He rinsed his arms and legs before dunking his head into the cool pool of water, letting the rest cascade down over his shoulders.

He returned to his seat. Perhaps sensing my malaise, he spoke of how often those he encountered seemed embroiled in some kind of forced march. He watched as countless pilgrims stopped to take the occasional photograph, but otherwise quickly sidestepped anyone who got in their way. He seemed saddened that the vagrancies of the pilgrimage – the bugs, the heat, the blisters and such – played such a prominent role in his idle conversations with fellow hikers. Shaking his head, he went silent.

I was struck by his insights and chastised myself for concentrating so much energy on the physical discomforts of the Camino, rather than its transformative possibilities. Whatever he was looking for, he seemed to have found. Being in his presence was like sitting with the Buddha. Had he not been rolling cigarettes, I might have concluded as much.

When our chatter waned, he gathered his things and left. As he did, an elderly man from the village approached me. He had been watching the two of us. Seeing an opening, he hobbled over, supported by two gnarled wooden canes.

The temperature was scorching, and yet he was wearing a long-sleeve shirt, vest, pants, and a hat. When he got closer, I could see his canes were wrapped in twine. A gob of string attached a handful of items to his walking poles; a soda can pull tab, a stone, and a few feathers splayed in various directions. He stopped in front of me and began to speak rapidly in Spanish. After hearing him repeat the word "Maria" a few times, I thought he must have mistaken me for someone else. I took off my ballcap and slid my sunglasses on to the top of my head so he could see I wasn't she.

Undeterred, he just smiled. Then, leaning heavily on his left cane, he raised the right stick and gently tapped me on one shoulder and then the next. During this anointing, he held my gaze so intently it made me blush. And then, without another word, he turned and left.

Afterwards one of the townspeople told me he was the village shaman. All of his interventions were done in the name of the Virgin Mary; hence the repetition of the name Maria. The particular ritual he performed on me was meant to dispel a bad memory, taking it from my shoulders and transferring it to his stick. He said the shaman was careful never to touch anyone he was trying to heal. His canes allowed him to absorb whatever sadness was lingering, and then transmit its energy back into the ground, where it belonged.

Maybe that was why walking the Camino was so hard. The dirt had absorbed so much sorrow and had been watered by so many tears. In return, it punished those who rained such torment upon it.

I went back to the hostel somewhat befuddled by the afternoon's events. Sascha and I returned to town to see if the only bar had opened. It had not, but there, parked in the middle of the road, was a large truck. Inside the vehicle were 10 computer terminals, all powered by a giant generator. Everyone was allowed 30 minutes of free internet access. Only on the Camino, I thought.

We both vaulted up the short ladder and into the flatbed, logging on to our email accounts. When our time had elapsed, we headed back to the bar only to discover the owners weren't going to open at all that evening. Back at the albergue, I pulled out half a loaf of bread, slathered it with peanut butter, and topped it off with a few apple slices. I split my crusted concoction with Sascha, thankful we had stored away a few morsels for just this sort of situation. Seeing our meager portions, our hosts prepared two plates of risotto for us. Although it was covered in red pepper garnish, I cleaned my plate. It was an unexpected end to what had been quite an unusual afternoon.

But my streak of good fortune ended abruptly that night. In an effort to keep my insect bites to a minimum, we closed both the door and the window in our small bunkroom. In short order, the heat became stifling. Dry and hot, it felt like we were in an oven. I crept out of my bunk and made my way out to the courtyard of the hostel. To my relief, it was significantly cooler there. I found an old leatherette couch and carefully laid down, trying to be as quiet as possible.

For much of the night, the noise from the street kept me awake. I heard bottles smashing. I was privy to a raucous argument between lovers. At 2:00 a.m., the front door opened with a creak. The hosts of the albergue had returned. I held my breath, hoping they wouldn't notice I had relocated to the lobby. Luckily, they both strode by, oblivious to my darkened shadow. I stayed until just past 4:00 a.m., not wanting to be discovered by an early riser. It was an awfully short night.

As dawn rose over the horizon, I carefully surveyed each limb. Red welts now covered much of my arms, legs, stomach, neck, and feet. When the tally of bites reached 100, I stopped counting. Having served nobly as the blood bank for the insect population of northern Spain, I now began to wonder, where was the shaman when I needed him?

Tea and Crumpets

"Be master of your petty annoyances and conserve
your energies for the big, worthwhile things.
It isn't the mountain ahead that wears you out – it's
the grain of sand in your shoe."

—Robert Service

Time to pay the piper.

Yesterday's retreat meant we had no other choice but to start our day by hiking the hills. A daunting prospect so early in the morning.

If the route to Astorga was traced on a piece of graph paper, it would look like a gigantic "W." Starting at the peak of Alto Santibañez, we embarked on a treacherous downward slope toward the banks of the Río Lagunas, followed by a steep climb to the crest of Alto Santi Toribio. Once back in the clouds, we descended again, and then shifted gears back up the slant to Astorga, a journey of some 7 miles (11.2 km).

During the daybreak's slalom course, I added petulant to the list of adjectives that could be used to describe my mood. As I labored to traverse the trail's contours, I was acting as if the Camino owed me something. Dirty, itchy, and sweating,

I seriously began to wonder if I even wanted to finish what remained. It was a thought that filled me with equal parts dread, relief, and shame.

A slideshow began to flicker in my head, filled with the kind of colorful images that were splashed across the pages of L.L. Bean catalogs. You know the ones. Where fresh-faced 20-somethings sport their "Be an Outsider" t-shirts, amidst the most spectacular scenery, all while modeling trail pants that clung to their slim hips and firm thighs. This, I can assure you, was not *that*.

And then came Astorga. It was nothing short of dazzling. Bustling with people and cheerfully painted storefronts, it was an oasis within the vast and endless stretch of red clay and rubble that for days had surrounded me. At the far end of town was the Palacio Episcopal, a neo-Gothic gem designed by famed Spanish architect Antoni Gaudí. It loomed over the city's expansive plaza like a Disney castle. A stone's throw in the other direction was the town hall. Its clock tower featured two animated figurines moving to the delicate plink of chimes. I felt like I had been dropped into a snow globe, where everything was crisp and bright and jaw-droppingly beautiful. I pulled my camera from my pocket and pressed it to my cheekbone, angled for the preparatory one-eyed squint. But the viewfinder did the scene no justice. This was a moment best captured by memory alone.

Sascha was waiting patiently in the plaza of our new wonderland, armed with a warm croissant and a cold bottle of Coca Cola he had purchased for me. With my "breakfast of champions" now in hand, we sat down on a nearby bench to take in the view.

We debated the pros and cons of ending our day right there. The scenery was inspired and the streets were brimming with activity. At the far edge of town, the trail headed back into the mountains, which meant dropping temperatures, an increased chance of rain, and a steep climb. Daunting though that was, we had only walked 7 miles that morning. I didn't want the next day to wipe us out and made the case that we should push on to Murias de Rechivalda, tacking on an additional 3 miles (5.3 km) that afternoon. This would make the next day's journey to Rabanal a reasonable 10-mile (16.1 km) hike, including an elevation change of nearly 850 feet. Walking a few extra miles today could make a world of difference tomorrow.

In the end, we agreed to continue. But not before lingering for a spell on the plaza. I bought an additional soda and banana for the road, neither of which lasted to Murias. I needed those calories to make it to our next destination. When we finally arrived, my host rewarded me with a stamp for my Compostela and a tall glass of ice water for my throat.

It was love at first sight.

I must have drawn the short straw once again, as I found myself bedded down next to a man whose snoring literally shook our bunk. Annoyed by the racket, the man in the adjacent cot took the opportunity to joust him with his walking stick, despite not knowing him. But even that did little to quiet the rumble. Lying atop his sleeping bag, wearing only the smallest of underwear, he wheezed and snorted his way through the remaining hours of darkness while the rest of us steamed.

Bleary-eyed and sleep-deprived, Sascha and I stumbled out of the doorway of the albergue on the early side, eager to get a jumpstart on the day's climb. The route took us through two relatively deserted towns, Santa Catalina de Somoza and El Ganzo. There was something disconcerting about passing through these crumbling villages, something that made me want to tiptoe in deference to the ghosts of the past. Perhaps it had something to do with the string of small wooden crosses I discovered. Each was woven into the wire fence that bordered the trail. They were fashioned from a combination of wood, leaves, and stones. Their presence made me feel as if I were walking through a graveyard.

Rabanal reported to be a town of 20 residents. On most days, that meant pilgrims outnumbered townspeople, something that became evident when we strolled down the main street. After yanking ourselves up the last few miles to this mountaintop nest, we were greeted by a gaggle of other hikers. I had read about a small hostel that was run by the London branch of the Confraternity of St. James. Eager to trade the customary glass of sangria for a cup of tea, we made our way to the appointed address. I crossed my fingers there was still an empty bed or two.

In a strange coincidence, the couple who welcomed us to the hostel had also processed our request for a Compostela many months back, while we were still in the States. When summer rolled around, Rosanne and Gene relocated to Spain to serve as volunteers at the albergue in Rabanal. Stationed at the front desk, they were quick to recognize our names when we presented our paperwork. They inked our pilgrim's credential and then handed each of us a fitted sheet and pillowcase, all in a hermetically-sealed packet. This act of germless sterility was just the kind of hospitality I craved.

A bell rang at precisely 5:00 p.m., calling us to tea. Sweet and hot, each cup of this British elixir was served with two stout digestive biscuits. As I bathed in the Anglo familiarity of it all, Gene amused me with stories of his own research on the Camino, including a passage he discovered in the autobiography of President John Adams. It told of his walking the main street of Rabanal on January 4, 1790. David McCollough's biography on Adams also made note of this. The Camino certainly made for some interesting bedfellows.

My mind, flush with the saccharine intoxication of Earl Grey tea, felt surprisingly serene. Sitting on my other side was the husband of the other host couple, a veterinarian named Daigle. Although outside the sphere of his traditional pool of patients, I asked if he wouldn't mind taking a peek at my bites. After an intensive examination, he declared that bed bugs, and not fleas or mosquitos, had been the culprits.

He gave me a multi-page handout on the topic, and urged me to wash and dry everything in my possession at an extremely hot temperature. That was the only way to rid myself of the infestation.

I hadn't been bitten by bugs while walking through multiple locations, as I had thought.

I had been carrying them *with me*. Good Lawd.

I chucked the whole lot, including my pack and sleeping bag, into the hostel's washing machine and pressed "HOT." Then the pile cycled for over an hour in the dryer. My clothes were a bit tighter by the end of it, but at least they were free of passengers.

We got an early start the next day, partly to get a jump on what would be a long and arduous climb, and partly to rid ourselves of the pot-bellied German in the tiny underwear who had been our bunkmate for a second straight night. Two women, LoLo from Japan and Kay from Korea, were at the sink brushing their teeth when I entered the communal bathroom that morning.

In between spits, the first said, "Last night was a snoring symphony."

The other replied with a similar exasperation, "And my bunkmate was the conductor!"

Good Friday

n. The Friday before Easter.
The anniversary of the crucifixion of Christ.

Quicksand

"The world breaks everyone, and afterward, some are strong at the broken places."

—Ernest Hemingway

Cruz de Ferro, the highest elevation on the Camino

Cruz de Ferro. Cross of Iron.

Three hundred and fifty miles of walking will bring you to the Cross of Iron, the highest point on the Camino de Santiago de Compostela. Today we would reach the zenith of our pilgrimage.

Cruz de Ferro is located 4,934 feet (1,504 m) above sea level. This meant the morning climb would involve an additional ascent of nearly 1,200 feet. Concerned about the difficulty this task presented, we left the albergue before the sun had even risen. It was so dark I could barely see the path ahead of me. With eyes glued to the trail, I made my way carefully and slowly up the dusty red lane that led out of Rabanal.

The rise lived up to its billing. It was very steep and very treacherous. But once again, the most difficult part of the experience was being hounded by a fleet of insects. Gnats, flies, and mosquitos congealed together to form a black cloud orbiting my head. Not to be outdone, one lone pest spent the entire morning darting between my mouth and eyes, all the while filling my ears with its incessant buzz. By this time, the monotone hum of insects had even begun to invade my sleep. There was no escaping their perpetual drone.

Inside. Outside. Morning, noon, and night. It had become the soundtrack of my pilgrimage experience.

The higher altitude thinned the swarm a bit. Then, in the distance, I got my first glance of the cross. It sat high atop a tall slim pole. At the base was a pile of stones, a substantial mound that encircled the bottom of the pillar. Higher up, other items had been attached to the wooden spire. This collection included a hodgepodge of mementos, including photographs, handwritten notes, and faded ribbons fluttering in the breeze.

Just 100 yards from the trail's pinnacle, I stopped. Crossing this threshold was a moment I wanted to share with Sascha. I would wait.

As soon as I saw him round the corner, a lump rose in my throat. I couldn't seem to catch my breath. Tears welled up in my eyes. In the long shadow of that cross, I began to weep.

Everyone who heard of my plan to walk across Spain asked me why. Some asked in jest, at first not realizing I was serious. Some were suspicious, as if my motivation was some sort of indication of instability or folly. Still others asked from a place of ardent curiosity, expecting the reply to be less of an answer and more of a revelation.

Over the course of the last 350 miles, I too had asked nearly everyone I met this same question. What brought you here? What was so compelling that it wrenched you away from your life of comfort and deposited you here on this lonesome trail? Much to my surprise, almost everyone gave the exact same answer.

My heart is broken.

Some were in the throes of a divorce. Some were mourning the death of a parent. Some had found themselves abruptly out of a job. Some longed to revive the relationship they had once enjoyed with their children. Some ached for their youth. Some had had their world shattered by alcohol, or drugs, or were the victims of sexual violence.

When I first considered walking the Camino, I didn't recognize any of these kinds of somber undercurrents in my own motivation. I saw the pilgrimage as an adventure, something that would push me to the very edge of my physical capabilities. Like anyone embarking on a marathon, I considered only the distance to be traveled, not the depths to be explored.

But like quicksand, the Camino had caught me unaware and ill-prepared, swallowing me whole before I even knew what was happening. Just a few steps in and I was already drowning in feelings of grief, contrition, and regret. Right up to my neck.

Seeing that cross, both a symbol of crucifixion and a beacon of hope, overwhelmed me. As sweat and tears streaked my cheeks, I realized the Camino had finally broken me.

And then, like a rogue wave, a deluge of images began to wash over me. And with them, a cacophony of emotion.

The exhaustion that comes from running away from who you are and what it means.

A lifetime of hiding in plain sight. Ears always piqued for signals your secret might be discovered.

The anger and fear that is part and parcel of inhabiting a female body; trapped by a reproductive cycle marked by birth, blood, and barrenness. Too often made to live by someone else's rules. Your own genesis forever tied to a discarded rib.

But it was not these "isms" that felled me at the foot of the cross that day. Not the undercurrent of homophobia I experienced nearly every day. Not the cultural, ecclesiastical, political, or economic constraints of sexism. It was something much more personal. Something much more incendiary. Something I likely shared with each and every pilgrim I had met.

Loss. Plain and simple.

The death of my father. The time I had wasted. The lingering backwash of my childhood; pangs I most often experienced as survivor's guilt.

The sorrow of a failed marriage. Love affairs gone awry. Regrets and disappointments, rooted in failures of both omission and commission.

CeCe's suicide had certainly stirred this smoldering pool of lava. But I had needed the Camino, in all of its monotony and struggle, to unearth it completely. The hills, the heat, and the endless stretch of miles were all necessary ingredients of this illuminating concoction. The only piece of the puzzle I was missing was the spark. That is … *the act of walking.*

There is a magic to ambulation. It is something I first learned during those long jaunts I took on the beaches of my youth. In fact, it has been my one consistent practice when I need to clear my mind or plunge the depths of some emotional quagmire. There is just something about the kinetics and rhythm of walking that slows everything down just enough to make it manageable, enough to exorcise the anguish from even the deepest crevices of my heart.

I had never before taken it to this extreme. The pounding my body endured during the hundreds of miles I had traversed cracked every protective wall I had ever erected. And now, every ghost who haunted me, every nightmare that lingered, every fear or moment of self-doubt I had ever experienced – they were all on full display.

And it brought me to my knees.

But here's the thing. By the time you reach middle age, your once lithe and malleable body has begun its inevitable decline. Crow's feet and gravity have firmly taken hold. And no amount of water, or moisturizer, or yoga can keep your neck from wrinkling or your hair from turning grey. But along with this same aging comes scar tissue, often much stronger than the original flesh it has replaced.

When I was younger, I saw the world in black and white. Right and wrong. For me or against me. In those days, my confidence was frequently tinged with an exaggerated sense of self-righteousness. I had all the answers back then. I was vigorous but not flexible. Strong but brittle.

What I didn't fully appreciate back in my salad days were the countless ways in which I would grow *stronger* with age. I bend now. I play the long game. Like the very iron of the cross at which I knelt, I have been made more formidable by the impurities that mark my life.

Getting older is no joke. And I wouldn't have it any other way.

In that moment I knew, without a shadow of a doubt, even as the tears fell from my lashes, that I would finish the Camino.

My crying jag, initially borne of fatigue and frustration, was also laden with gratitude, and relief, and *pride*. I had made it to the highest crest of the ridge. I was indeed stronger in all the broken places.

One of the traditions of the trail was to leave some sort of memento at the cross. It was usually an item the pilgrim had carried from home. A stone. A photograph. A letter. Some sort of tangible representation of what had brought him or her to the Camino in the first place.

The most popular item left were rocks, symbolic I assumed of a burden finally laid to rest. Sascha and I had no such offering, so we scrambled up the jumble of loose rocks in an attempt to get close enough to touch the base. Now just an arm's length away, I could actually see the faces in the pictures and read the handwritten messages. Some had been tacked to the wood with nails. Others were held by string. It was a tattered collage, equal parts anguish and love. Simultaneously beautiful and stunningly heartbreaking.

Compelled to be part of this collective prayer, Sascha and I mused about what we should leave. In the end, he pulled a small sheet of blank paper from his journal and wrote the words *Non Sibi* (Not for Self). Folding the scrap into a small triangle, he tucked the message in between the others affixed to the beam.

These two words were the moniker of Phillips Andover, the place where our lives had intersected, our shared institutional love. As always, he had managed to strike the perfect tone.

Just the right sentiment at just the right moment.

Easter was coming. It was all downhill from here.

Pentecost

n. the Christian festival celebrating the descent
of the Holy Spirit on the disciples of Jesus
after his Ascension.

Gods of Fútbol

"So God blessed the seventh day and hallowed it,
because on it God rested from all the work that he had
done in creation."

—*Genesis 2:3 (NSRV)*

Casillas. Hernandez. Ramos. Villa.

This foursome is FIFA's version of the Beatles. Heroes of the young and the envy of the old. Outshone by only Matthew, Mark, Luke, and John in this most Catholic of countries. But not today. Today the World Cup belongs to Spain.

After soaking in the panoramic view that stretched outward from the Cruz de Ferro, Sascha and I began the perilous descent to the mountain village of Acebo. For a second time, I untied Beth's walking sticks from the back of my pack and used them to brace myself against the disappearing slope. I skidded across the ground's surface like an awkward grasshopper, wincing as my toes jammed forward in my hiking shoes. By the end of the day, my nerves were fried and my knees and feet were battered.

I plopped down on the nearest bench as Sascha went to investigate the housing possibilities. Perhaps sensing my fragility, he settled on a small double room with a shared bath, located conveniently and centrally over the town's bar. The only store was right next door. Before heading up the stairs for the night, we bought two ridiculously enormous tomato and cheese sandwiches. It was going to be a take-out night for us.

Perched on the room's balcony, I absentmindedly watched as a line of pilgrims streamed by on the street below. And then I saw him. *Snoring man.* He was no longer carrying his pack, which meant he must have already secured lodging in Acebo. Thank the Lord Sascha hadn't chosen for us to bunk at the albergue that night.

Over dinner, we discovered we had both experienced a "first" that day. For Sascha, it marked the first time someone had passed him on the Camino. He admitted to being both embarrassed and amused that the speedster in question was a 50-something man. Adding insult to injury, he told me the guy was also pulling a large wheelbarrow behind him. A double ding to Sacha's pride.

For me, it was my first "full fanny" sighting – unwittingly coming upon someone with their pants around their ankles, in the midst of "having a moment." Like Sascha, I think I was more embarrassed than anything else. Certainly more embarrassed than was my fellow traveler.

Eventually our conversation drifted toward more important topics; in particular, where we should stop the next night, the night of the World Cup final. The town of Ponferrada was just under 10 miles (15.7 km) away. With a population of over 60,000, it was a former medieval stronghold, and now served as the capital of Spain's El Bierzo region. It would be a short day's hike, but we wanted to be in as big a town as possible for this last game against the Netherlands. Most weekends were quiet on the Camino. But you could already feel the buzz in the air.

Tomorrow was going to be something special.

We left Acebo just after 6:00 a.m., passing a ghostly sculpture of a riderless bicycle on the way out of town. It was a tribute to a fallen pilgrim, killed while riding the path. We had come across other such tributes during our time on the Camino. Much of the trail was rural and remote, far removed from any sort of medical facility. It made me wonder how many hikers became injured or stranded while on the pilgrimage, without the care they might need. Once again, I was reminded this was not an undertaking without risk.

The rest of the morning was spent negotiating the dip into Molinaseca, a quaint outpost I appreciated all the more for the toast and jam I enjoyed while stopped at their local café. My Dad was right. Bread is a gift from the gods.

Re-fueled once more, I hiked a long and steady uphill before coming into a grassy flat. A cluster of young boys raced across the field, operating a fleet of remote-controlled model airplanes. They were joined by a donkey, a shepherd and his sheep, and a group of old men carrying a variety of brass instruments and drums. The band members were all dressed in matching blue shirts and pants, topped off with festive straw hats. Every so often they would stop and set off a bottle rocket, much to the collective delight of those gathered. Except for the sheep. Those poor sheep.

A shepherd and his flock, on the grassy plains of the Camino

In celebration of our successful arrival, and conscious of wanting to be some place a bit more secure if the Spaniards won the Cup that night, we made our way to the front desk of the Hotel Los Templarios. The room rate was reasonable and the hotel offered plenty of air conditioning. Best of all, it was just a short walk from the main plaza.

After wolfing down a few slices of pizza, we headed to the center of town just after 7:00 p.m. A huge screen had been erected on one side of the square. Hundreds of chairs were lined up for the anticipated crush of spectators. Some residents had even dragged their couches out into the street.

A crowd of people had begun to gather. Women with their cheeks painted in lipstick, a red/yellow/red stripe drawn across the bridge of their noses. Boys darted in and out of the assembled throng, trailed by Spanish flags they had pinned around their necks. The mob grew more raucous as the alcohol flowed. Sascha, God love him, sat next to me and read a book, unperturbed while the game thrashed on. Even the rowdy cheers and angst-ridden groans of the horde weren't enough to peel his eyes away from the page. He had come to keep me company. And keep me safe. I marveled at both his concentration and his loyalty.

It was a hard-fought first half. The score remained tied at nil. The undercurrent had shifted enough that I thought it best to watch the second half of the match within the confines of our hotel room. At the end of regulation, the deadlock remained. This was the case for the first overtime period as well. And then, just a few minutes before penalty kicks would be assessed, midfielder Andres Iniesta shot the ball on a hop past the sprawling Dutch goalkeeper. For the first time in history, Spain had claimed the Cup.

Pandemonium broke out in the streets. Fireworks streaked across the sky. Yelps and screams filled the air. And sots, arm and arm with their mates, stumbled up and down the alleyways until the wee hours of the morning, singing some kind of unintelligible celebratory chantey.

On this Sunday, every prayer had been answered. It was a hallowed day. All kneel to the gods of fútbol.

Haight-Ashbury

"How did it get so late so soon?"

—Dr. Seuss

It had been a while, but the tract ahead of us actually looked flat. With spirits bolstered, we decided to throw caution to the wind and set our sights on Villafranca del Bierzo, just over 15 miles (24.5 km) from the day's start line.

I arranged to meet Sascha in Camponaraya, the first town of note on our map. When I couldn't find him, I moved on to Cacabelos. After waiting an additional 30 minutes at this next stop, I began to grow concerned. This was a part of the Camino experience with which I often struggled. Living in an age of instant and constant communication meant being "out of touch" felt both strange and disquieting. If patience was a virtue, I was gaining ground toward canonization with breathtaking speed.

As I neared Villafranca, Sascha finally caught up with me on an uphill slope. He seemed totally unaware there was even something worthy of my worry. Apparently, I needed to embrace my "let go" mantra with a bit more conviction.

Villafranca lay roughly 120 miles (193 km) east of Santiago, on the border of the mountainous, sometimes rainy, and every so often snowy, Galicia region of Spain. The climb to the top of nearby O'Cebreiro is one of the most arduous of the entire trek. Many a pilgrim has fallen short of reaching the summit, stymied by the weather, the physical conditioning required, or both.

Precipitation and the vertical rise notwithstanding, we had another problem. Sascha and I were running out of time. I had made my roundtrip plane reservation without actually knowing how long this journey might take. Since parting ways with Jess, Meredith, and Beth, the two of us had covered an additional 196 miles. We were closing in on our goal, but given our truncated timeline and the upcoming terrain, there seemed little hope of arriving in Santiago on schedule.

Before we attempted to solve this problem, we decided to make a side trip to the town's chapel. Back in the day, Villafranca was known as "the other Santiago." Pilgrims unable to continue to the cathedral due to illness or fatigue received a blessing here in the local church, just as they would have had they been able to walk the pilgrimage in its entirety.

The Church of Santiago, a 12th-century Romanesque mission, beckoned the weary traveler through the Puerta de Perdón (the Door of Forgiveness). Once inside the threshold, a statue of St. James stood watch. Scallop shells act as wall sconces and an eerie red cross is projected onto the floor of the middle aisle. Votive candles imbue the darkness with a warm glow. As I slid into the back pew, a sense of peace came over me. After a few crazy days, the silence and serenity felt tangible enough to taste.

Later on, Sascha and I checked in to the funky Ave Felix hostel. It had a groovy Haight-Asbury kind of feel, with folks standing by to offer pilgrims healing oils or even read their Tarot cards. At the front desk, we were assigned two different sleeping lofts. When I balked, I was told the Felix offered only single-sex quarters, even for families. I wished Sascha luck, secretly relieved to have a night away from the snoring gaggle of men bunking down next door. Sometimes, it's good to be a girl.

A line of black rain clouds formed during my nap, a foreshadowing of the nasty weather to come. Now more than ever, we needed to devise an alternative plan. Rain in Villafranca often meant snow atop O'Cebreiro. Loathe though I was to consider it, a short bus ride seemed like the best option. Since this would involve crossing state lines, a multi-ride transfer was also required.

This transaction called for the kind of linguistic aptitude neither Sascha nor I possessed. After catching the correct bus to Piedrafita, we discovered the subsequent leg to Sarria was serviced by a bus that departed just once a day, at 6:45 a.m. We were officially stranded.

Deposited rather unceremoniously on the side of the road, we donned our ponchos before strategizing about next steps. As far as we could figure, we had four options: 1. follow signs to O'Cebreiro on foot, stay the night at the top of the mountain, and catch a bus from there the next day; 2. hitchhike; 3. take a taxi, assuming we could find a taxi; or 4. find a place to stay and make sure we caught the right bus at the crack of dawn the following morning. In the end, we both cast our vote for option number four.

We found a hostel near the bus stop, took showers, and had a leisurely breakfast. Having lost another day of walking, we would need to commit to a more up-tempo pace for the rest of the pilgrimage. The albergue provided access to the internet, so I shot a few cursory emails to Beth, hoping she could rearrange our hotel reservation in Santiago. She was able to do just that, extending our stay on the back end to account for our altered itinerary.

We crossed our fingers that whenever we managed to make it to our final destination, a hotel room would be available. This was not a given. Every year, the Feast of St. James drew huge crowds to Santiago. During the years when the feast day fell on a Sunday, as was the case this particular summer, the numbers grew exponentially. Swarms of tourists, pilgrims, and townspeople were due to arrive in Santiago for the impending celebration on July 25th. Knowing this, I had purposely made the decision to complete the pilgrimage and leave Santiago by July 20th, well ahead of the burgeoning throng.

With only seven days left before our deadline, the clock was ticking.

The Countdown

"Intolerance is the most socially acceptable form of egotism, for it permits us to assume superiority without personal boasting."

—Sydney J. Harris

After we waited on the edge of the road in the pre-dawn darkness, our bus appeared at the appointed time. Sascha and I both sighed in unison, grateful and relieved. We hopped aboard and then spent the remainder of the trip trying to hold on to our sloshing stomachs as the vehicle made its way up and over O'Cebreiro. It was a white-knuckle ride from stem to stern.

By the time we reached Sarria, a steady rain had begun. The streets were now teeming with hikers; school groups, tourist companies, college students, even young families on vacation. They were all so exuberant and so very, very clean. I, on the other hand, looked like something the cat dragged in.

Back in Boston, I had stuffed into the bottom pocket of my pack a fresh pair of underwear and a clean bra and t-shirt. This pristine collection had been carefully sealed inside a Ziploc® bag for the entirety of our trip. Knowing I would, at some point, be seated next to some unsuspecting soul on my return flight back to the United States, I thought it was the least I could do for my fellow passengers.

I had made a vow, before the trip began, that if I ever made it to Santiago, I would burn my clothes in favor of the items stowed away in my secret sandwich bag, retiring my membership in the great unwashed. But for now, I looked pretty raggedy compared to the majority of my fellow pilgrims.

At Sarria, we were pushed off the bus rather brusquely. Without knowing which way to go, we retraced our route, as I had remembered seeing a yellow scallop shell on the way into town. Once we found the sign, we were again on our way. But not without stopping to take a photograph, just as we had done the day we spotted our very first marker, back in Pamplona.

A long set of stairs brought us into the center of town, but it was difficult to follow the path after that. The yellow arrows were few and far between. Or perhaps they were just hidden behind the swelling crowds. Whatever the reason, I felt my mood begin to shift, as did Sascha's. We had walked hilly terrain, withstood the cold and wet, and survived more bug bites than I cared to count. The conditions were not the problem now. No, it was the deluge of people that got us off kilter. Our pilgrimage had suddenly morphed into what felt like a destination vacation.

The crowds dwindled as we reached the outskirts of town. In Morgade, we stopped at a small stone chapel. It was routinely used by those on the pilgrimage as a place to leave messages for fellow hikers. Once inside, we ran into LoLo, our Japanese friend we had last seen at Acebo. She had lost track of Kay at that point, and was walking with someone else. Nonetheless, seeing a familiar face made a big difference. It made the Camino feel like it was mine again.

Before leaving for Spain, I had come across a description in one of the guidebooks about the unspoken hierarchy that existed between hikers. It warned would-be pilgrims of taking a prideful stance when it came to engaging with their compatriots, specifically those who had traversed far fewer miles. And now, I too had fallen into that trap. I was annoyed by all the newbies, jamming up the trail, *my* trail. When they complained about the weather, or their blisters, or of feeling tired, it took all my self-control not to roll my eyes. *Seriously?* I thought. *You think this is difficult?* On the outside, I was deferential and sympathetic. But on the inside, I was in full-on brat mode.

It didn't take a rocket scientist to figure out what was really going on. Despite having walked more than 300 miles, I remained defensive – dare I admit ashamed – of the segments of the pilgrimage I had spent riding the bus. In fact, I was *still* kicking myself for starting in Pamplona, a mere 27 miles from the official start at St. Jean Pied-de-Port. It made me feel like a poser. Instead of just letting my journey evolve in its own way, instead of being grateful for what I had accomplished, I found myself judging the sojourns of my fellow pilgrims.

Good Lord, Anne, I thought. *What the hell is wrong with you?*

Our hike that day was only 10.8 miles (17.5 km), but it included going up and over Alto Páramo, some 200 meters higher than Sarria. Once on the far side of the peak, we came to the town of Mercadoiro, with a recorded population of one. It seemed an unlikely place to stop, but Sascha had heard the host of the village hostel was a delight. So, in we went.

As we crossed the threshold we spotted Jane, the British woman we had first met on the Meseta. She was hoisting a large glass of wine to her lips, surrounded by other Brits equally enamored with their potent potable. That sealed the deal. We would stay at Mercadoiro and join Jane in toasting her 62nd birthday.

During the celebratory dinner that followed, she introduced us to the clan of folks she had been traveling with during the past week. Glenys and Gary, a husband-and-wife team from Australia, a third Aussie named Hildegard, a woman from France named Marie Christina, and a Danish hiker called Brita. It was a tight squeeze to get all of us around the table, but worth the effort. Glenys and crew managed to bake a small cake for Jane. We sang multiple rounds of "For She's a Jolly Good Fellow," and enjoyed a delicious bowl of lentil soup, courtesy of our doting host.

It was amazing how just one evening of camaraderie affected me. True, I enjoyed the solitude of the Camino, perhaps more than I had initially imagined I would. But rubbing elbows with some familiar faces at the end of a day lifted my spirits substantially. Somehow the Camino had become one big Venn diagram, bringing all of us together at just the right moment. Like shooting stars, we had crisscrossed into each other's orbit. The magic of the Camino was, once again, on display.

As it turned out, I would need that emotional boost – the following day threw a worthy gauntlet of challenges my way. After crossing the bridge at Portomarín, following a truly ghastly descent, I promptly got lost. Unable to get my bearings or find any markers, I climbed more than 50 stairs in an attempt to get the lay of the land. Thirty minutes later, I finally spied a small yellow arrow. It got me back on track, but I was now unsure whether Sascha was in front of me or behind me. Every so often I would stop and wait, but still no Sascha. When Jane and the others passed me, each inquired about his whereabouts. We were all flummoxed. For the first time in quite a while, I grew worried I might not be able to find him before nightfall.

Up, up, and up I went as the rain poured down. I had lost some weight by this time and my pants were becoming loose. Now they were also soaked, and so heavy they began to slip down, catching the cuff under the heel of my boots. The splattering of mud on the hem made the pant legs even heavier. I grabbed the waistline with both hands to keep my trousers from sliding off my hips. If it wasn't so annoying, it would have been hysterical.

On the bright side, my snail's pace allowed Sascha to catch up. He had taken his time during the day, ducking in and out of the rain to avoid becoming waterlogged. The previous night, Gary had told us about an albergue named Casa Molar in the town of Ventas de Narón. It had gotten rave reviews. With so many hikers on the trail, Sascha volunteered to pick up the pace and hold a place in line for both us. Off he scampered.

The clouds began to dissipate as morning turned to afternoon, casting rays of sun down onto my shoulders. It was going to take more than that to dry my pants. I hoped this fantastic albergue lived up to its reputation.

Heading into the home stretch, I could see a crowd had gathered outside the door of our appointed hostel. Jane and the Aussies were keeping Sascha company. They had all arrived early enough to find a place at the front of the line. Which meant I had a bed for the night and plenty of company for dinner.

After showering and washing our clothes, we moved to the front patio; to write, to chat, and to turn our faces towards the sun, enjoying the sudden return of summer temperatures. It was so warm that Yolanda, one of the Dutch women who had joined our group, took the opportunity to do some topless sunbathing.

Just when I thought I had seen everything on the Camino.

For the second night running, we all had dinner together. It was loud and fun and turned into a second party for Jane. No one seemed to mind, least of all the birthday girl.

The next day the rain returned with a vengeance. I'm not sure if it was due to the weather or just a blessing from God, but miraculously, the onslaught of pilgrims had disappeared. Once again, I was alone with my thoughts.

My thoughts and their steady companions, the raindrops.

Ubi Caritas

"Clear eyes, full hearts, can't lose."

—Coach Eric Taylor, *Friday Night Lights*

In the pre-dawn darkness, I could hear the rain despite not being able to see it. Anticipating another soggy day, I rolled my pants into Camino capris, threw my poncho over my head and backpack, and lurched out of the albergue looking like a miniature camel.

The day's summit came and went in the first 30 minutes of the hike. Topping out at 2,262 feet (720 m), the climb to the peak of Sierra Ligonde got my blood pumping. It is reputed that Charlemagne stayed in Ligonde during the medieval heyday of the Camino. While normally enamored with these sorts of historical tidbits, I found myself distracted that morning by a conversation I had had earlier with Sascha. During the previous few days, he had grown uneasy with some of our fellow hikers. He sensed an anti-gay sentiment beginning to emerge, and although it was limited to just a certain faction of the group, he found it both disturbing and unsettling.

Getting into a rhythm with folks on the trail can be both a blessing and a curse. The "all for one and one for all" camaraderie that blossoms during such difficult undertakings can be inspiring. I had enjoyed being part of the development of our new nascent tribe. I had relied on them to help me with my daily route planning. I looked forward to being surrounded by familiar faces at the end of the day. It was a bond that made the Camino feel far less lonesome.

But, at times, it also felt like I was back in junior high school. Everyone was vying to be part of the "in crowd," to be invited to sit at certain tables, or to share inside jokes. It was a discouraging development.

Not surprisingly, as we had gotten to know one another, differences in culture, political views, and upbringing began to reveal themselves. Like in every "family," the squabbles soon followed.

That night was another raucous affair, with all of us once again landing at the same spot by day's end. Wine and stories flowed freely. Jane even regaled us with a tale about meeting Prince Charles at Windsor Castle. It was so much fun, until it wasn't.

As the night wore on, I grew weary of jokes that seemed more like barbs than jocularity. The quips had become a bit too pointed; the atmosphere a bit too sophomoric. I decided it was time for some fresh air.

I left the albergue and wandered over to a nearby church after hearing music wafting from across the street. Inside the Romanesque walls of the Church of San Tirso, a group of pilgrims was standing in a candlelit circle singing *Ubi Caritas*. I was mesmerized by the soft and yet insistent pulse of their Gregorian chant. I felt my heartbeat begin to slow and my shoulders relax. As I dropped into an open seat, I let the flicker of light and the fugue-like music wash over me. Over and over, the group chanted the refrain *Ubi Caritas*, translated as "where charity and love are, God is there." In the hushed darkness of that church, I realized charity was exactly what had been lacking over the course of these past few days. In me.

Likely the most famous line ever attributed to St. Paul is 1 Corinthians 13:13, "And now faith, hope, and love abide, these three; and the greatest of these is love." It had been uttered at nearly every Christian wedding I had ever attended, and yet, few realize that the love St. Paul speaks of in this well-known stanza is actually best translated as *charity*. Romantic love, filial love, even obsessive love get plenty of airtime in our contemporary culture. But charity is often the bridesmaid and never the bride when it comes to grasping the brass ring of virtues, always overshadowed by its sexier half-sister.

And so it was with me. Far too often, charity was an afterthought, instead of my initial approach. Which is odd considering the lucky star under which I had been born. Sure, I had hit some icy patches during my childhood and adolescence. Who doesn't? But I had also grown up with parents who loved me, and who had done their very best to give me every possible opportunity. I had a cadre of friends who were forgiving enough to see past my less-than-stellar moments. Their loyalty and affection have remained steadfast, despite my occasional churlish behavior. They are my chosen family, my foundation, and my safe harbor.

I have even been blessed to find someone who cherished me with an abiding devotion I sometimes feel I don't deserve and often don't understand. Whatever Beth sees in me, she does with an enormously charitable heart.

With a pang of guilt, I came to acknowledge this shortcoming while bathed in candlelight that night. For far too long, I had depended on good manners and an ability to hold my tongue to keep others from discovering just how judgmental I could be, how impatient, how haughty. Those flaws, cleverly disguised, were viewed by others as my striving for excellence, as having high standards. What better way to hide my fussiness than to disguise it as aspiration?

By that point, the grind of the Camino had dulled my polished veneer. The weaknesses I fought so fiercely to conceal were gleaming with clarity. Sitting in that pew, I could see how my own disapproving tendencies had thwarted my progress, spiritual and otherwise. Even if I had managed to fool everyone else, I couldn't fool myself.

Ubi Caritas. Where *charity* and love are, God is there. Somehow, I needed to move charity into the center of my heart.

If the climb to the Iron Cross had been the emotional apex of my pilgrimage, this moment was my nadir. But in the best possible way. It would be from this place, this painful flash of self-discovery, that I would launch the next portion of my life.

I learned so many lessons while on the Camino. Some more substantive than others. But coming to terms with this particular Achilles' heel was more illuminating than I had imagined possible. I suppose truth-telling always is.

The journey to Santiago, equal parts grueling and transformative, had broken me in a way that was necessary in order to rebuild. Now it was time to put the pieces back together.

"Let go," I prayed. "It's time to *really* let go."

Slowly I stood and crossed back over the marble threshold into the cool night air.

I was finally ready for the Camino to end.

The Finish Line

"There are years that ask questions and years that answer."

—Zora Neale Hurston, *Their Eyes Were Watching God*

We were now just 50 miles from Santiago.

Having scouted the day's route the previous night, I awoke anticipating a day of relatively flat terrain. Nothing could have been further from the truth. What looked like small nodules on my map were actually substantial. The heat was searing and, for over 10 miles, I saw not one building nor one fountain. It was complete desolation.

Near the end of the day, I came across Hilde, part of the Australian contingent. She had fallen well behind her mates due to the onset of a bad case of shin splints. We made a motley couple, she and I, each step accompanied by an audible wince. Suddenly, like a mirage, a hostel appeared, flanked by a wide and deep river. We got two of the last six bunks that were available and collapsed, reserving a third bed for Sascha. My knees and feet ached from the strain of the day's hike. For two hours, I didn't move a muscle.

As the sun slid down toward the horizon, I gingerly made my way back to the river bank. Comprised primarily of snow melt, the water was absolutely frigid. I clenched my teeth and lowered both legs into the gushing current, right up to my thighs. When numbness replaced the throbbing, I exited the water, my legs so stiff they felt like wooden stilts. Staggering across the grassy expanse, I headed back inside.

Hilde and I both mistakenly rose at 5:00 a.m. the next morning, thinking it was an hour later. Under the bathroom's fluorescent light, we soon realized the error of our ways. We snuck back to our bunks hoping to catch a few more winks. Forty-five minutes later, I awoke to Hilde whispering in my ear, "I'm ready!" Time to go.

Sascha and I had agreed to make Santa Irene our next stop, just under 12 miles (19.1 km) from our starting point. Much of the day we walked through old growth forest, infused with large swaths of eucalyptus trees. All morning I hiked with the faint scent of Vicks® VapoRub™ in my nose.

When I reached the appointed albergue, Sascha convinced me we should soldier on another 1.9 miles (3.1 km) to Arco do Pino, just 12.5 miles (20.1 km) from Santiago. These additional miles would guarantee this would be our last night on the trail. The remaining segment was a gentle downward slope. I put my pack back on and off we went.

For weeks I had scoured the path ahead of me, looking for telltale yellow arrows or scallop shells that would confirm I was going the right way. Just before entering Arco, I came across a sign that simply said "Santiago." It didn't display a directional arrow or any further explanation. Someone had cheekily scrawled across the bottom in chalk, "Thanks for reminding me. I had forgotten."

A spontaneous guffaw erupted from my belly.

By the end of the hike, the heat was intense enough to make me feel woozy. This was exacerbated when, after crossing into town, we saw nearly a hundred pilgrims waiting in line to secure a bunk at the public albergue. Luckily, there was a newly renovated private lodge on the top of Arco's main thoroughfare. Lowering our heads, we made one last climb. When we reached the front door, it was as if we had followed the yellow brick road straight to Oz.

Everything was spotlessly clean. An enclosed glass courtyard allowed streams of sun to illuminate the middle of the lounge. Our additional effort was well rewarded. With only a few people ahead of us, I was enjoying a cool shower within minutes of my arrival. If I had to rank all of the places we stayed while on the Camino, this hostel would grab the top spot.

All night long, the excitement of the imminent completion of the pilgrimage was palpable. The next morning, before the clock had even struck 6:00 a.m., Sascha and I stumbled out into the dark. Turns out we were the last to leave. Everyone else had already bolted.

At the town border, the path led us into a deep and very dark grove of trees. Sascha dug through his pack until he found Beth's old headlamp. We followed the shaft of light for quite a while before making our way through a short tunnel and back up to an asphalt road. When we stopped for breakfast at San Payo, we had already walked 2.4 miles (3.9 km) and the sun hadn't even risen.

During those early morning hours, I found myself moved to tears. I wondered what was behind my sudden sentimentality, strange now that we were so close to accomplishing our goal. But this was how I often experienced my crying jags, spouting just as often from sadness as from happiness, from anger as often as from nostalgia.

By midday, we had arrived at the summit of Monte de Gozo, elevation 1,214 feet (370 m), the final rise on the pilgrimage trail. It was literally all downhill from here. From this vantage point, the spires of the Cathedral were visible. My tears had, by that time, been recast as a wide and toothy grin. A long gentle slope sprawled before us, the gateway to Santiago.

Most of the folks we had been walking with over the course of the past week were also milling about on top of Monte de Gozo. We decided we would walk the final miles together – one last hurrah before being caught in the crush of pilgrims entering the great stone plaza of the cathedral.

The outskirts of Santiago were strikingly unremarkable; filled with storefronts, small homes, and quite a bit of traffic. The physical beauty of the Camino's landscape had disappeared from sight. As had the medieval charm we so often experienced in the rural meanderings of the trail. Each time I looked up, hoping to catch a glimpse of the famed cathedral, I saw only pavement and construction sites. In fact, it was only during the final stretch that the streets narrowed and the city was transformed back to its historical and architectural roots.

I heard someone yell my name. Scanning the crowd, I saw the British couple who ran the albergue in Rabanal on the sidewalk – ironically the same pair who had processed my original request for a pilgrim credential while all of us were still back in the States. They were the first to welcome me, joyously and robustly, to Santiago.

The finish line was just ahead. But having been welcomed and recognized, *by name*, brought my pilgrimage to a symbolic close. I eagerly bounded over to them, hugging both as tightly and fiercely as I had anyone in my life. The remaining blocks to the cathedral were a blur.

A few more turns and we rounded the final corner, spilling into the Praza do Obradoiro, the large square that ringed the cathedral. From high atop the central tower of the westward-facing façade, a statue of St. James stood watch. While the grandeur of the church was remarkable, the vast pedestrian plaza surrounding it was surprisingly subdued. Only a handful of pilgrims drifted about, taking photographs and walloping each other on the back. Beneath the soaring spires and sturdy turrets, there was precious little activity at ground level. My journey ended not with a bang, but with a whimper.

Feeling a bit flummoxed by the underwhelming reception, Sascha and I decided to make our way to the Oficina del Peregrino, located adjacent to the cathedral. Here we would receive our official certificate of completion. Upon arriving, we discovered Jane, Glenys, Gary, Hilde, and Yolanda already in line. Now reconnected with our fellow comrades, the excitement of finishing quickly returned.

The clerk carefully inspected my credential, covered with stamps from numerous albergues, and concluded I had indeed walked a sufficient amount to be considered a true *peregrino*. He painstakingly inked his name to the bottom of my certificate. After tucking the paperwork into a protective cardboard tube, he told me I would be recognized at the Mass scheduled for the following day. My name would stand among the thousands of others on their official records. I had walked my final mile.

After a deliciously long night's sleep, the next morning Sascha and I ambled out into the twisting alleyways of what was the medieval hub of Santiago. Within a few minutes, we ran into Evelyn. She had finished two days earlier, hiking the last few miles with Eileen. Just around the corner, we discovered Glenys and Gary sharing a quiet moment, huddled over two steaming cups of coffee. We waved from afar, letting them enjoy their breakfast in peace.

My plan for the day included just three things: touring the cathedral; attending the noontime Mass; and finding an internet café where I could let friends and family know that Sascha and I had arrived safely to Santiago. Much to my surprise, Sascha decided to forego the cathedral, including the celebratory Mass. He wanted to shop for some new clothes. I couldn't blame him. I too was tired of wearing the same two items I had donned for over a month. But it was more than that. If I wasn't clear on his motivations before, I was now. Sascha had walked all of this way *for me*. He had walked so I could walk, and not because he had any particular interest in experiencing or completing the pilgrimage. The cathedral, the pageantry, even the relics of St. James were all just window dressing for Sascha.

He had walked the Camino as an act of love.

With a wad of cash burning a hole in his pocket, Sascha headed to the stores while I made my way to the cathedral. For a good stretch of time, I puttered around the cavernous interior, just trying to take it all in. The confessionals were doing a brisk business, but I sidestepped the growing lines and headed to the Portico de Gloria, an ornately carved column containing the famed Tree of Jesse. It was considered a rite of passage for pilgrims to offer thanks for their safe journey by pressing their hand into this decorative edifice. But hundreds of years of this practice had worn finger holes deep into the stone. Concerned by the wear and tear, the display had been subsequently covered with a glass plate. Holding my palm against the protective shield was as close as I was going to get.

At the far end of the church was the altar, flanked by a monstrous golden backdrop. Gilded in gold and silver, it was both garish and radiant. To the left was a set of stairs. After climbing the twisting steps, I found myself near the top of the baroque canopy. Carefully balancing myself on a small platform, I peeked over the shoulder of the gigantic statue of St. James down to the main floor of the church. It was customary for pilgrims to ascend these stairs and then wrap their arms around the figure's shoulders. I followed suit, resting my forehead on the back of the sculpted neck of the famed apostle. Unnerved by a brief moment of vertigo, I pressed my torso firmly into the bejeweled mantel of the statue. It was all a bit surreal.

There was a separate set of stairs that led to the crypt, located directly beneath the altar. Here I found the small silver reliquary containing the remains of St. James and two of his disciples, St. Theodorus and St. Athanasius. A small kneeler was attached to the bench facing the display. After descending into this narrow passageway, I knelt at its wooden railing in silence, worlds away from the hundreds of pilgrims wandering the church floor just above me.

By this time, it was close to noon and many pilgrims and tourists had begun to find seats. After finishing my prayer, I made my way back to the main floor of the cathedral. I squeezed into a pew just to the right of the altar, in what is referred to as the transept. During the service, it would be across this perpendicular portion of the church that the *botafumeiro* would travel. This thurible expelled huge plumes of incensed smoke as it flew across the church. It was the most dramatic part of the daily worship service.

Soon every nook and cranny of the building was filled with people. As part of the opening of the service, a deacon approached the lectern and read a list of those who had just completed the pilgrimage. Although our names weren't read individually, I thrust both of my arms skyward when he declared two pilgrims from the United States had successfully walked from Pamplona to Santiago. This outburst clearly startled the other people in my pew. No matter. I had to celebrate.

At the end of the Mass, eight men stepped onto the altar and began to loosen the knotted ropes of a side column, lowering the *botafumeiro* from near the ceiling to within reach. Once it was filled with incense, they lit it, clamped the top back on, and began to rhythmically pull opposing ropes so as to start its swing.

The thurible slowly began to move higher and higher. At its height, it hurtled through the air at close to 40 mph (64 kph). I watched as it careened over my head with each yank of the rope, leaving huge clouds of smoke in its wake, only then to streak back across to the other side of the transept. The choreography of it was spectacular and done with amazing skill and precision. It was the most fantastical bit of liturgical showmanship I had ever seen.

In earlier times, the burning of incense was as much a ceremonial act as it was a matter of health. Pilgrims often brought to the cathedral questionable hygiene habits and, at times, disease. Dousing them with smoke once inside the church was one way to combat the odor of both. But now, the *botafumeiro* was largely a symbolic feature, appealing to pilgrims of every faith and station.

Once back outside, I meandered over to the main fountain, the prescribed meeting place for Sascha and me. He was already waiting, clad in a bright white button-down shirt and a fresh pair of khaki shorts. The shopping trip had obviously been a success.

James, Evelyn, Eileen,
the author, and Sascha
(from left to right) in Santiago

Much to my delight, Eileen, Evelyn, and James were also waiting with Sascha. All ravenous with hunger, we set off to find lunch, order a glass of wine, and snap a few pictures. It would be our last hurrah.

Eileen and Evelyn decided to walk to Finisterre the next morning. This outcrop of rock is at the western edge of Spain, the closest point of land to the United States. It is literally the "end of the earth," giving way to the great expanse of the Atlantic Ocean. Only a handful of pilgrims travel the additional 54 miles (87 km) from Santiago to Finisterre. But for Eileen and Evelyn, the journey continued.

James planned to return home. Yolanda, Glenys, Gary, and Hilde were still unsure. Brita's progress had slowed considerably and she had not yet reached Santiago. Perhaps I would see her again. Perhaps not. Just as easily as we had come together, we now came apart.

That night, with mixed emotions, I wrote my final email blast to both friends and family. The time had come to move on.

July 20th

After ...

37 days
355 miles walked (and an additional 79 by bus totaling the requisite 434 from Pamplona)
a half a bottle of Advil
62 cans of Coca Cola
too many flea bites to count
and just ONE blister ...

it is finished. We have touched the granite and marble façade of the Cathedral of Santiago. We are officially pilgrims of St. James.

Both Sascha and I received our Compostela, our certification of a completed pilgrimage. Today at the Noon Mass they announced to the throng of thousands that two pilgrims from the United States had completed the pilgrimage, beginning in Pamplona. From a faraway pew I raised my arms in triumph, much to the stares of the others in my row! I was swept up in the smoke of incense, billowing out from above the crowd, swinging precariously from a container hovering near the ceiling. It is otherworldly.

On the small cobbled streets of Santiago, we have now run into all of our Camino pals from the past month - crazy Evelyn, Irish Eileen, our Australian-Dutch-Brit contingent, James the New Orleans seminarian, Francie from Germany, everyone is here celebrating alongside us.

More tomorrow, after some sleep and a long hot shower.

¡Buen Camino!
SAG

Alone Time Together

"Every long lost dream led me to where you are
Others who broke my heart, they were like northern stars
Pointing me on my way into your loving arms
This much I know is true
That God blessed the broken road
That led me straight to you."

—Rascal Flatts, *Bless the Broken Road*

The author and her wife on the trail outside of Pamplona

When Beth and I first started dating, I launched into a soliloquy one afternoon about the differences between introverts and extroverts. Don't get me wrong. I love Beth's vivacious demeanor. She talks to everyone. She knows everyone. She even loves everyone, as far as I can tell. Beth is the classic extrovert, gaining energy with every conversation and every interaction.

She is the queen bee around whom others hover.

I, on the other hand, recharge in solitude. While I enjoy being surrounded by people, I often choose to watch rather than participate in the cacophony that swirls around me. I crave time for more isolated pursuits, like curling up on the couch to read, or driving through desolate landscapes, or taking early morning walks along the ocean's edge. I am the classic introvert, rejuvenated by the absence of conversation or interaction. I stand off to the side, taking it all in, before retreating into my shell to make sense of it.

It isn't that I want to be alone necessarily, or that Beth constantly seeks chaos. But we often joke I would be happiest living a life of complete anonymity in New York City, while she is best suited to being the mayor of Mayberry, RFD.

We are living proof that opposites attract.

But as every extrovert/introvert combination knows, in order for the relationship to thrive long-term, both people need to understand and appreciate the gifts of their complement. It was with that in mind that I initiated a tête-à-tête one day about our distinctly different emotional styles. Beth listened with acute concentration as I began to extoll the intricacies of life as an introvert. As my diatribe continued, I danced carefully across the high wire known as "alone time." I had found this concept created much consternation with previous extroverted partners, many of whom viewed it as self-indulgent, a strategy of purposeful avoidance, or worse.

With the deft touch of a surgeon, I tried to explain how "alone time" wasn't something I invoked to punish or distance myself, but rather a way for me to revitalize. Spending time by myself, I assured her, wasn't a signal of impending doom. It was part of how I managed being in a relationship. As if straight from the script of some sappy afternoon special, I heard myself say, "It's not you. It's me."

When I finally finished my monologue, Beth waited a moment or two. Then she cocked her head ever so slightly, nodded ruefully, and said, "Can't we just have our alone time ... *together?*"

Her response was as sincere as it was ridiculous. And yet I was completely smitten by its earnest simplicity.

You know what, I remember thinking. Maybe we just could.

After my divorce I had stumbled, badly, through a handful of relationships. Each began in exhilaration, as new romances do. But each ended painfully, some leaving me so broken I wondered if I would ever truly recover. While my friends tried to reassure me there was still "someone out there for me," more often than not I experienced this well-intentioned salvo as a hollow platitude. Couldn't they see I was reeling? And the thought that someone would just waltz into my life – my middle-aged, somewhat pudgier, and increasingly messy life – seemed highly unlikely.

And yet, that was exactly what happened. The friend of a friend, Beth first met me on a one-sided blind date; that is to say, she had seen me, but I had not yet seen her. After exchanging a few emails, thanks to an introduction by our shared chum, we agreed to meet one Thursday night for a quick dinner. I got there on the early side and found a spot to sit, just to the left of the podium used by the restaurant's hostess. Beth would certainly recognize me, I surmised, so there was no need to query everyone in the lobby as to their identity. I would just be patient and wait.

Soon enough, a pretty blonde came bounding in and headed straight for me, flashing her signature grin as she approached. Without warning, I felt all the air go out of my lungs. Then a thought, just one thought, crowded everything else out. *Where have you been all this time? I have been waiting for you …*

And so, for the past 18 years, we have had our "alone time together." Not literally in the sense that we spend every waking moment in each other's company. But rather, that we have found a way to stride side by side; sometimes together and sometimes separately, but always pulling our oars in the same direction.

Ours is not a young love and I wonder if this has made things easier. We brought to the union an undeniable accumulation of wrinkles and scars, and checkered histories we may still regret but have given up hiding. At our age, it is time for authenticity, not pretense. For the very first time in my life, I had found someone with whom I felt completely comfortable, completely myself.

I could finally let my guard down. I was home.

Even so, approaching Beth about joining me on the Camino was a "big ask," as the saying goes. But I think she sensed it was important to me at the very deepest of levels. Growing up in the Roman Catholic church, I located my spiritual life within the time-honored rubrics and rituals of liturgical practice and theological homogeneity. Not only did the aesthetic appeal, but the conviction that being a person of faith required acts of charity, mercy, and justice made sense to me. It's not a coincidence that the Catholic Church has birthed so many hospitals, schools, and charitable organizations. Theirs is truly a model of faith in action.

As I grew older, the conservative theological and cultural views of the church of my youth began to chafe. Despite assurances to the contrary, I no longer felt wholly welcomed and cherished by my faith community. It was an experience that caused me significant pain and a wellspring of remorse. In the end, and despite my longstanding allegiance, I left. I just couldn't find a way to stay.

Many years later, I discovered the Episcopal Church. I rejoiced at finding a tradition so similar to the one in which I had been raised, but with a much more progressive political, cultural, and theological lens. As a lover of words, I delighted in the increased attention paid to the biblical text and to preaching, and found myself quite taken with the exquisite language of the Book of Common Prayer. The Episcopal tradition places great value on the life of the mind and the importance of intellectual inquiry. Within this milieu, my spiritual life blossomed anew.

I feel blessed to have had my vocation recognized without regard to my gender. I am grateful that my marriage is not only tolerated, but celebrated within my faith community. And I have gained enormous strength and solace from the rich ecclesial tapestry into which both my personal, and now professional life, is woven.

And yet, walking still remains the most cherished implement within my spiritual toolbox. It clears my mind. It soothes my nerves. It opens my heart in a way that no other discipline or practice ever has. Not even close.

When I was a child, both of my parents impressed upon me what a gift it was to be able to move with ease. My father, hampered by the loss of his leg, spent the vast majority of his life disabled. My mother, stricken with polio while very young, lost a good portion of bone in one ankle. As a result, her feet did not grow uniformly, causing one to be significantly smaller than the other. She too endured a life constricted by a lack of physical mobility.

Both made due, as children of the Depression often did. But I have no such physical limitation.

I am *free*.

Instead of being satiated by my journey on the Camino, I find myself even more fervent to walk the world. The fields, the hills, the rocky crags, and edge of the sea, all beckon to me like sirens.

Someday, God will call me back out into the wild. And I will go …

Epilogue

"A time it was, and what a time it was, it was
A time of innocence
A time of confidences

Long ago it must be
I have a photograph
Preserve your memories
They're all that's left you."

—Simon and Garfunkel, *Bookends*

Writing this book has been an emotional rollercoaster. Even now, all of these years later, the memories of this adventure live in my mind in dazzling technicolor.

I imagine it might be of interest to some of you to know what happened to all of the characters who wandered in and out of the previous pages. So, for all of you, a glimpse into that crystal ball …

Then and Now

<u>"Chicago,"</u> aka Mary Catherine (then, 66 years old).

I remember asking "Chicago," after a number of days of walking together, whether she might ever return to the Camino. "Life is short," she replied flatly. "There are too many other places to see. No, this is a 'one and done.'"

True to her word, she now counts Rome, Israel, Knock, Borobudur, Prambanan, Potala, Lourdes, and various other cathedrals and shrines among her pilgrimage experiences. "I walked because I am an adventurer," she remarked, "always desiring a challenge. And I walked this particular path because my Catholic beliefs and connection to the Divine draw me to sacred zones."

It took her just 32 days to reach Santiago. A week after returning home, she moved from Illinois to Indiana in order to homeschool three of her grandchildren. In 2016, she moved once again, this time to State College as her grandsons brought their considerable wrestling skills to Penn State.

After each has been bestowed his tassel and gown, she hopes to move someplace a bit warmer. As she wryly noted to me in a recent email, "I am, as of this missive, awaiting inspiration on a specific direction."

I learned something from each person I met while on the Camino, no utterance more impactful than "Chicago's" aptly named "one and done" rule. I too have now ascribed to this worldview, hoping my own adventures will be as rich and varied as those of my fellow pilgrim from our nation's Heartland, one of the very few Americans I met while on the Camino.

Godspeed, "Chicago." A woman of both faith and devotion.

<u>Eileen</u> (then, 46 years old)

In 1982, well-known Vietnamese monk Thích Nhất Hạnh co-founded a Buddhist monastery in southern France named Plum Village. It was to this peaceful hamlet that Eileen, as well as Evelyn, ventured after completing the Camino. Her time there gave her an opportunity to begin to process her experience of the pilgrimage, a peaceful lily pad on which to rest.

She and Evelyn have remained in contact, becoming such close friends that they returned to Spain the following year to walk the Camino del Norte, an adjacent route that hugs the northern shore of Spain's Bay of Biscay. In recent years, she has allocated much of her time to caring for her aging parents, in addition to tending to her own health issues, some severe enough to be considered life-threatening. It has been a difficult stretch for her.

But in typical fashion, Eileen remains hopeful. She planned on returning to Spain to traverse the Camino once again in 2021, a holy year on the pilgrimage's calendar. Her first attempt required 36 days from stem to stern. She knew her next bid would necessitate more time, and yet she remained undaunted. "It was a special time with special people whom God brought together for a short intense period of time," she wrote, reflecting on our time together in Spain. "I just knew at the time I had to walk ... and your email has reminded me I'm not going to die. I will live. And I will walk (again)."

To my Irish sister from another mother, your courage and determination inspire me. I pray our paths, whether in Ireland or in Spain, cross again very soon.

Evelyn (then, 58 years old)

Currently living in the greater metropolitan area of Vancouver, Evelyn has zigzagged her way across much of the globe since we hugged goodbye on the cobblestone streets of Santiago.

After extending her initial pilgrimage with a jaunt to Finisterre, followed by a subsequent hike of the Camino del Norte with Eileen the following year, Evelyn set her sights next on the Camino Portugués. This pathway begins in Lisbon and extends 382.5 miles (615.5 km) to Santiago's cathedral. Although shorter in distance, this avenue offers far fewer services and facilities. Only 13 percent of all pilgrims choose this option. Undeterred, Evelyn conquered this as well.

Her experience of the Camino altered both her personal and professional life. When the trip concluded, she began to study mindfulness, meditation, and yoga. These interests culminated in two separate periods of study in India, in addition to her time with Eileen in Plum Village. Now officially retired from teaching, she has designed and launched a pilot program on cultivating mindfulness in her former school district.

After years of parenting, caring for both her mother and mother-in-law, the lure of the Camino snuck up on Evelyn. Just two weeks after her youngest son graduated from high school, she found herself on a plane headed for Spain. "It was time to wander," she later revealed. "Our Camino was truly a turning point. I remember it like it was yesterday. It probably changed the direction of my life."

As it turns out, "crazy Evelyn" wasn't so crazy after all. For all you future pilgrims, I hope you find your Evelyn on the Camino, as I did mine. She was truly a ray of sunshine.

James (then, 25 years old)

As expected, upon returning to the United States, James entered the novitiate in hopes of becoming a Catholic priest. The process of discernment and training for members of the Society of Jesus (more commonly known as the Jesuits), is a long and arduous one. After spending the first two years of the novitiate in his native Louisiana, James went on to St. Louis to teach, followed by three years of study in Toronto (philosophy), and then a similarly long stint in Boston (theology). All of this will eventually lead to his earning a Ph.D., one piece of a fairly lengthy and complicated ordination puzzle.

Following a hiatus of nearly nine years, James and I recently had a chance to sit down over coffee. After a couple of hours of laughter and reminiscing, I asked him why he chose to walk the Camino. "It was the closing of a chapter in my life," he mused. "Once I entered the novitiate, I knew I would no longer be able to make unilateral decisions about what I wanted to do or where I wanted to go. I guess it was my way of saying goodbye to that part of my life."

Buen Camino, my friend. The church will surely benefit from your gentle heart.

Jess (then, 29 years old)

Perhaps more than any of the "Fab Five," the Camino provided Jess the time and solitude to make one of the most important decisions of her life. After returning from Spain, she and Jack got engaged and married quickly thereafter. And as it turned out, her fears regarding her ability to conceive went unfounded as she is now the mother of not one, not two, not three, not four, but *five* children. Once a panther, always a panther.

No doubt it takes every last ounce of her energy, creativity, and stamina to keep her brood all moving in the right direction. That said, there are few women I know who are up to this daunting task. But Jess is one of them.

And as if that weren't enough, Jess and her family spent four years of their children's young lives residing in Mexico City.

A glutton for adventure, she was on board when Jack accepted a job transfer. By then, with kids in tow and more on the way, she flung herself headlong into a new culture. She was far from home and without any knowledge of the language. This chapter was no easy feat for my dear friend.

During a recent visit, I watched as she and her kids scampered up the steep steps of the nearby Mayan pyramids. Who knew walking the Camino would be just a warm up for Jess?

She knew. That's who.

Now back in the States, Jess has made the stunning canyon landscapes of Utah her home. Every day is an adventure for she and her family. Just as she had hoped.

Meredith (then, 18 years old)

It's still hard for me to believe Meredith had only been out of high school for a month before setting out with all of us on this grand adventure. But thankfully, Meredith has always been an old soul. Her infamous plea to Beth, "I feel it in my heart," during that fateful day when both were forced to carry two backpacks, is among the most treasured moments of our time together in Spain. I marvel at her grace under pressure, even now.

Meredith spent her undergraduate years at Duke University, a place she loves with the rabid passion of every member of Blue Devil Nation. Despite a rather tepid initial interest in sports, she became a disciple of the great Mike Krzyzewski and began tutoring members of the famed basketball team during their off-court stints.

She now finds herself enrolled in medical school; a dream for as long as I have known her. Who better to enter this profession than this smart, thoughtful, and compassionate young woman?

To all her future patients, you heard it here first. Your body, your heart, and your soul will be in good hands with the soon-to-be Dr. Meredith.

Sascha (then, 18 years old)

Like Meredith, Sascha's post-Camino life began by enrolling in college. After a whirlwind three years at Tufts University, he relocated to Portland (OR), transferring a handful of courses from a local institution to keep him on track for graduation.

Then it was on to a position as a software designer for the municipality's water system. Shortly thereafter, his position was altered to include fieldwork, a designation that called for Sascha to wander the city's underground sewer system and swim its rivers. Not a job for the faint of heart.

That was followed by a stint as a data manager for a nearby research hospital, followed by completing a graduate degree in computer science. With another credential in hand, he moved to New York City before ultimately making his way back to the Pacific Northwest.

As part of his educational training, Sascha was required to teach. This facet of his program had a profound impact on him. "Teaching is the most engaging and rewarding challenge I have ever taken on," he declared. Given his intellectual acumen, patient demeanor, and kind heart, his future students are in for a real treat.

The time Sascha and I spent together on the Camino is one of my most precious memories. He is as close as I have ever gotten to having a son. And although he would balk at the suggestion, I certainly learned just as much *from* Sascha as he may have gleaned from me.

Isn't that always the way?

To all the rest – Brita, the "Dred Sibs," "Dublin," Frankie, Glenys, Gary, Hilde, Jane, Kay, LoLo, Marie Christina, Patrick, Tao, Yolanda, and the countless others who enriched my journey beyond measure, I remain so very grateful for your presence and companionship while on the pilgrimage.

The Camino lives on through the recollections I have of each of you. Until next time …

Buen Camino.

Acknowledgements

Walking the Camino changed my life. Writing about it changed everything else.

Both of these tasks demanded different kinds of support, all of which were essential in transforming this dream into a reality. On the equipment side, I am particularly grateful for the expertise of the staff at my local REI store. After a careful and thorough assessment, I was fitted with the right gear at the right price. They knew what I didn't, and prepared me for the specific challenges I would face on the Camino. In CamelBak, Keen, and Apex I trust.

I received financial support for this trip from a variety of sources, including the Abbot Academy Fund (operated under the auspices of Phillips Andover) and the Episcopal Diocese of Massachusetts. This generosity helped defray much of the cost associated with this adventure. Assisting in this cause were the always kind-hearted Elizabeth George and the Reverend Dr. Frederick Moser. My thanks to both.

When it came time to put pen to paper, a tribe of cheerleaders came to the fore. Chief among them, the members of my writing group – Nina Scott, Dr. Christine Marshall, and Dr. Andrea Bailey. The Tuesday evenings I spent at Nina's kitchen table, bolstered by this trio of women, were among the most joyful moments of this book's gestation. I was also the benefactor of a self-designed writing retreat in New York City, thanks to Philip Gerson by way of Eric Gutierrez. I am happy to report the big lights still shine brightly on Broadway.

Every author needs someone to take a chance on them. Ingrid Beck, you were that someone. You believed in this project, even in its nascent stages. You guided me through the obstacle-ladened process of preparing a book proposal, soliciting publishers, and the dreaded task of creating a "brand." Twitter and I are officially a couple, thanks to you.

I would be remiss without mentioning the countless editors who featured my work over the course of this past year, helping me gain traction with a wider readership. Cloe Axelson of NPR's Boston affiliate WBUR, you were the first in this regard. Who knew an article on the Grammy awards would have led to this? Olga Segura, I am humbled by the trust you and the other members of the staff at the *National Catholic Reporter* have given me. Progressive voices of faith, mine included, have found a home with you. Doug Sparks, you championed my work in our shared backyard, offering me multiple opportunities to gush about the hiking trails and other hidden gems of the Merrimack Valley. One day soon, promise me you and I will ramble the woods, bogs, and fields of the Bay Circuit Trail together. I would love that. Before I wrote about the Camino, I dabbled as a sportswriter. Bill Corey, thanks for adding me to your stable of freelance writers. I am a newspaper girl at heart, in the most old-fashioned kind of way. Covering baseball and horse racing for *The Providence Journal* was so fun it can hardly be considered work.

It's all well and good to write flowery descriptions of scenery and plumb the depths of one's heart with poignant prose, but what about grammar, and dangling participles, and serial commas? Honestly, this is *not* my strong suit. Luckily, I had a magenta-colored, pen-wielding wizard at the ready. With surgical precision, this transcript was vetted, corrected, and made infinitely better by the devotion and love given to it by Eileen Pollack. You made the nuns at Sacred Heart proud on this one, Palamino. Mr. Brown is indeed a farmer.

When I needed to infuse this book with a little flair, I knew just where to turn. Steve Rosenberger, your deft hand and creative vision helped put the frosting on this cake. If the devil is in the details, you my friend, you are a graphics diablo.

Prior to publication, I was offered the chance to speak about this experience at a variety of venues. Crafting these presentations went a long way in helping me discern how best to relay the inward and outward metamorphosis I experienced on the Camino. My thanks to MJ Engel for inviting me to speak at Phillip Andover's inaugural TEDx program. I am grateful beyond measure to Dr. Jack Jia and Shanghai's WLSA (World Leading Schools Association) Academy for the chance to appear as a guest lecturer as part of their faculty exchange program. It was an honor to partner with my old friend Dr. Michael Hanophy and the community of St. Joseph's College (Brooklyn, NY) as the keynote speaker for their annual Founder's Day series. Fairfield University (Fairfield, CT) rounds out this distinguished list. Designing a program to mark the fiftieth anniversary of co-education was always safe in the hands of Janet Canepa and Martha Haley. I remain proud to have been included among the list of speakers tapped for this seminal moment in the school's history.

None of the above would have even been necessary without the spirited sense of adventure brought to this journey by the other members of the "Fab Five." We were a quirky bunch, for sure. But all of you breathed life into this dream of mine, and in the process, provided the fodder for this text.

To "Just Go," "Go Slow," "Ami-GO," and "Go GO," I offer my profound love and gratitude. *Peregrinos* for a time, family forever.

And finally, for Beth. With you, anything is possible. Here's to a lifetime of spending our alone time together.

Notes

Cover image and all photographs courtesy of the author.
Chapter headings courtesy of Steve Rosenberger.

Chapter 3

1. Statistics provided by https://www.americanpilgrims.org.
2. Ibid.
3. Map courtesy of Steve Rosenberger.

Chapter 7

4. *The Holy Bible: New Revised Standard Version.* Oxford
   University Press, 1989.

Chapter 13

5. *The Holy Bible: New Revised Standard Version.* Oxford
   University Press, 1989.

Chapter 16

6. Livestream provided at http://www.irache.com/es/
   enoturismo/fuente-del-vino.html.
7. John Brierley, *A Pilgrim's Guide to the Camino de Santiago,*
   6th edition (Scotland: Findhorn Press Ltd, 2010).

Chapter 29
8. *The Holy Bible: New Revised Standard Version.* Oxford University Press, 1989.

Epilogue
9. John Brierley, *A Pilgrim's Guide to the Camino Portugués*, 5th edition (Scotland: Findhorn Press Ltd, 2014).

About the Author

Writer. Minister. Adventurer.

After spending twenty-five years working at two of Boston's premier educational institutions, Harvard University and Phillips Academy, Andover, the author currently leads the chaplaincy program at Harvard-Westlake, a private secondary school in Los Angeles.

Her debut book, And So I Walked, recounts her journey of traversing the 500-mile Camino de Santiago de Compostela. Using the famed pilgrimage path as a backdrop, Gardner's memoir weaves together her personal narrative with the physical, emotional, and spiritual challenges presented by the Camino.

Inspirational, and at times heart-wrenching, And So I Walked explores how faith, family, and friendship both change us and sustain us.

Follow her on Twitter @AnneGardner2020 or on her webpage at www.anne-gardner.com.